Henry Lamb

Out of the Shadows

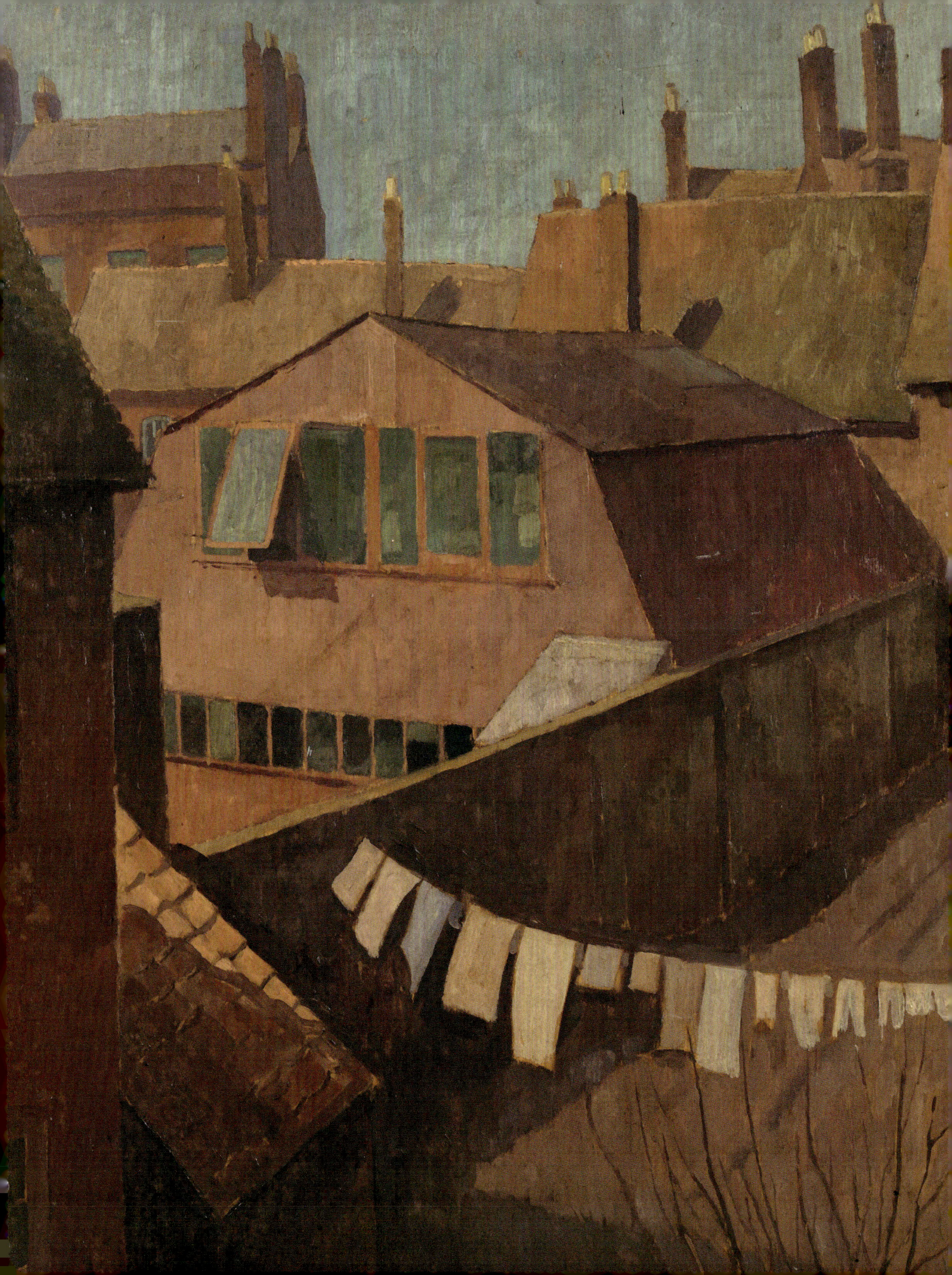

Henry Lamb

Out of the Shadows

Harry Moore-Gwyn

THE SALISBURY MUSEUM
POOLE MUSEUM
PAUL HOLBERTON PUBLISHING

This catalogue accompanies the exhibition

Henry Lamb *Out of the Shadows*

Salisbury Museum, Wiltshire
26 May 2018 – 30 September 2018

Poole Museum, Dorset
18 May 2019 – 29 September 2019

ISBN 978-1-911300-36-6

British Library Catalogue in Publishing Data
A CIP record of this publication is available from the British Library

Produced by Paul Holberton publishing
89 Borough High St, London SE1 1NL
WWW.PAULHOLBERTON.COM

Designed and typeset by Laura Parker
Printed by Gomer Press Ltd, Llandysul, Wales

FRONT COVER *Self-portrait*, 1914 (cat. 12), detail
BACK COVER *Paradise Street*, 1923 (cat. 23)
FRONTISPIECE *View from the Artist's Studio, Poole*, 1922 (cat. 24), detail
FACING *The Tea Party*, 1926 (cat. 27), detail

Supported using public funding by ARTS COUNCIL ENGLAND

RA250 1768-2018 Royal Academy of Arts with Art Fund

This project, with Art Fund support, forms part of RA250 UK: Exhibitions and events around the UK to celebrate 250 years of the Royal Academy of Arts

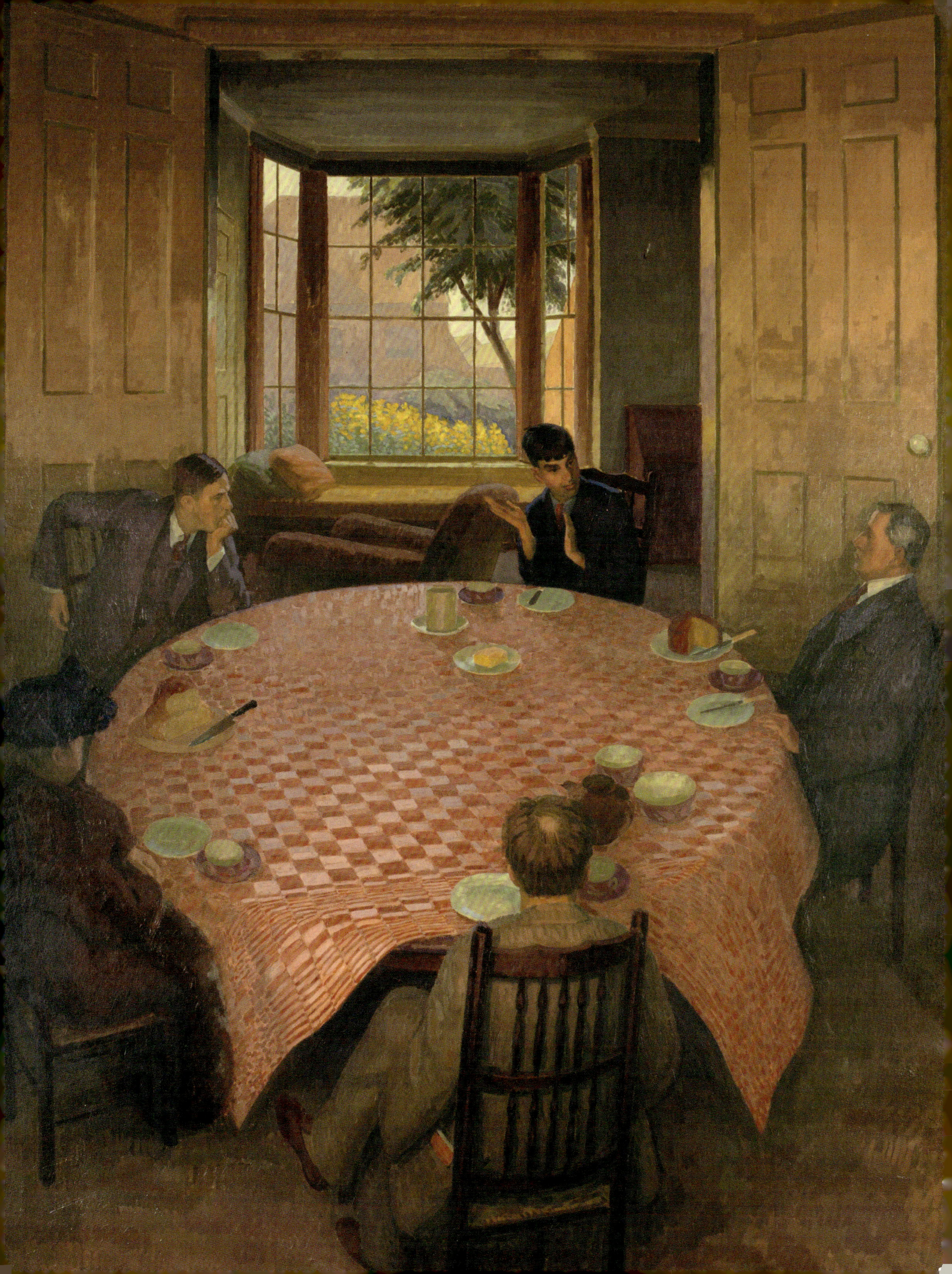

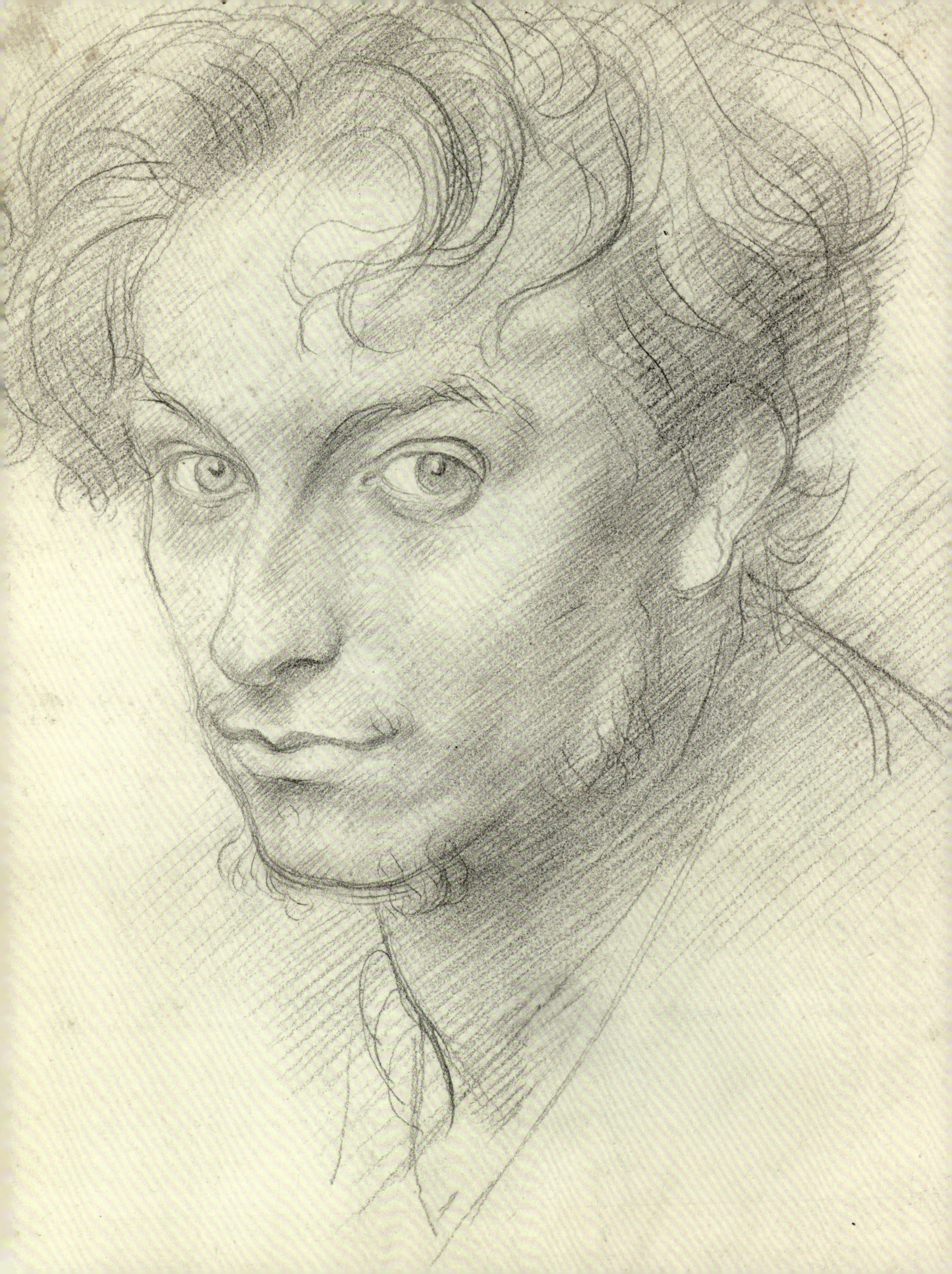

FOREWORD

Salisbury Museum's exhibitions programme reveals the stories about creative and talented people connected with the Wessex region. Many have been inspired by the outstanding heritage and landscape of the Salisbury area to create great works of art or literature. Over recent years our exhibitions have ranged from famous artists, such as John Constable, to others less so who deserve more attention, such as John Craxton. *Henry Lamb: Out of the Shadows* follows the latter.

Henry Lamb was one of the leading British figurative painters of the first part of the twentieth century. A close associate of Augustus John, patron of Stanley Spencer and friends with members of the Bloomsbury Group, he was also an accomplished musician and trained as a doctor. He served as a medical officer in World War I and was commissioned by the British War Memorial Committee to produce one of the leading commemorative pieces after the war (see cat. no. 14). He became a trustee of the National Portrait Gallery and of the Tate Gallery and a full member of the Royal Academy in 1949. Lamb came to live in the Wessex area in the 1920s, first in Poole and later, after his marriage to Pansy Pakenham, in Coombe Bissett, just south of Salisbury, which was his home for the rest of his life.

Lamb is an artist who is ripe for a reappraisal. Despite his prolific and skilled output he has not been the subject of a major exhibition since the 1980s. Therefore when independent curator, dealer and writer Harry Moore-Gwyn approached the museum with an exhibition proposal we were eager to seize the opportunity to revive interest in him. Harry was at the time working with Henrietta Phipps, Henry's eldest daughter (who sadly passed away in 2016), on cataloguing the Lamb family archive. Using the archive as the basis for the exhibition has offered exciting opportunities to link original sketches and drawings with finished paintings and exhibit previously unseen material. The result is a wide-ranging exhibition that covers the full remit of Lamb's career.

Out of the Shadows is a product of the newly formed Wessex Museums Partnership, which received Arts Council funding to become a National Portfolio Organisation in 2018. Salisbury Museum worked to create this exhibition with lead partner Poole Museum, where it will be shown in 2019. The partnership has also supported Poole Museum's major exhibition about Augustus John, which will run in parallel with *Henry Lamb: Out of the Shadows* and move to Salisbury the following year.

Salisbury Museum would like to extend its gratitude to Harry Moore-Gwyn for his work on the exhibition and catalogue. In addition we wish to thank the many museums and individuals who have kindly lent works to make this project possible, in particular the Henry Lamb Estate, who have been most generous in allowing regular access to the archive. Other major supporters of the exhibition have included the Paul Mellon Centre for Studies in British Art, who provided a publication grant; the RA250/Art Fund project, celebrating 250 years of the Royal Academy; and the Patrons of Salisbury Museum, who have helped fund this catalogue.

ADRIAN GREEN
Director, Salisbury Museum

FACING *Self-portrait*, c.1906 (cat. 1), detail

A Personal Recollection

MARK GIROUARD

Coombe Bissett 220
Salisbury
13/9/57

My dear Mark
It was very good to hear from you even with the quite maddening news of the shirt. Is it in the hands of someone in Schloss Schwartzenberg? & can't it be disgorged in time for our next sitting. Your good will about that prospect is most gratefully noted. I forget if I told you how the undemonstrative Henrietta allowed herself some superlatives about the picture. The likeness. Only a certain nebulosity on your shoulders needs to be dispelled: but such things are so subtle and relative that I always find myself completely relying on having all the original data before me – when I resume.

Having seen in the Pakenham publicity press (Foreign Daily Mail) about Thomas in the care of his Saint, I wrote to him there: but haven't heard a word, and when I rang the hospital in London this week I was told that he was discharged. I would rather have heard they were keeping him for another month of test meals and modern interioscopes.

I forget if I told you we arrived from France on 5th after many misfortunes. I went to London for 3 days work this week – standing at a gaudy & ambitious picture of a don from Durham: I managed to advance it substantially, but I think the effort was premature, for my R leg seems now completely crippled.

Val [his son Valerian] *is due home – from Germany! – late tonight and goes shooting in Hereford on Monday.*

I have signed on for 23 more sittings Sept 25 and 26 from my Don. By that time I may be able to function again if not to attend the lecture of Dr M. Girouard at Courtauld. In any case I am looking forward to some comparing of notes about foreign travel: & if you can bring some of your collaboratrices, so much the better.
With love from Pansy [his wife Pansy Pakenham]

Yrs, Henry

I HAD BEEN STAYING WITH MY FRIEND ERKINGER Schwarzenberg at his parents' house in Tuscany. My clutch of letters from Henry almost all date from when he was painting my portrait, commissioned by my father in 1957. I had got to know him a few years previously, through his daughter Henrietta, a first cousin of my friend Thomas Pakenham – we were all at Oxford together.

Henry was nearly fifty years older than me, smallish and wiry, and when I first knew him still remarkably agile, apart from increasingly crippling arthritis in his hands. When we went on walks together he hopped over gates or dived through hedges with the greatest of ease. We became friends, and I had no feeling of any difference of age between us. We just got on very well together. Although he talked, as he wrote, with a slightly old-fashioned formality, he was not at all stiff as a person. He was quite without pretension or showmanship, which is not to say that he did not have very strong likes and dislikes. As with many artists, his dislikes included almost all art critics and art historians.

I don't know why he and Pansy Pakenham, when they married in 1928, settled at Coombe Bissett, a few miles from Salisbury. They lived in a square, early nineteenth-century house of moderate size, with the river and Henry's studio at the bottom of the garden. The house was vaguely Bloomsbury in feel, painted rather than wall-papered, in undemonstrative colours – the external woodwork blue-green if I remember rightly. Henry never invited me into his studio, and I don't remember any of his pictures hanging in the house, though I suppose some of them must have been. Much the most powerful object in it was Stanley Spencer's great painting of the Centurion's servant, dying on an iron double bed in a Cookham attic. Henry never talked to me about his friendship with Spencer, which had long ago been discontinued.

A sad feature of the drawing room was the spinet, made for Henry by Tom Goff, the one, I think, on which he used to play duets with Augustus John's wife Dorelia, now standing disused because of the arthritis in his hands.

His dislike of Augustus John was evident. He imitated

to me with relish John, as he once overheard him, when painting a portrait of a child, and after the parents were well out of the way: 'Keep still, you little toad, or I'll tear your guts out'. John's own children he had been very fond of, and he was in love with Dorelia for many years. I don't remember him talking about Lytton Strachey. Once, when for some reason we had got talking about homosexuals and heterosexuals, he said that he thought most people had a bit of both in them – perhaps he was thinking of his friendship with Strachey.

Lewis Dodd, in Margaret Kennedy's *The Constant Nymph*, is supposed to have been modelled on Henry, although it is also said that they were barely acquainted. I have to say, though, that Dodd seems to me exactly how Henry might have been, forty years or so before I knew him.

He didn't seem especially dug into Wiltshire; he painted nothing there to equal his series of pictures of Poole, painted when he was living there in the 1920s. I don't think he frequented the local pubs, but he had no great desire to be in with the local nobs, either, though they were very willing to be in with him. Once, when, out walking (not with me), he saw the car of the Radnors from Longford Castle approaching, he dived into the ditch to avoid recognition, and did not emerge until it had passed. Country-house life never meant much to him (though my first visit to Cranborne Manor was when taken to tea there by him and Pansy). In the 1930s, along with tribes of Pakenhams, Evelyn Waugh etc., he went a good deal to stay with Pansy's brother in Ireland, but all he ever told me about life at Pakenham Hall was the thrill of seeing the succulent forearm of Pansy's sister Julia stretched out on the green of the billiard table. For him, his most memorable Irish days were when he stayed and painted on Gola Island, off the coast of Donegal, in 1912. He told me about the beauty of one of the fisher-family daughters, and what a bitter let-down it was when she came to London and he went to see her, and found her encased in a nurse's uniform, and wearing glasses.

Henry painted my portrait in London, not Wiltshire. He had a studio flat in Roland Gardens, South Kensington, and came up to London fairly regularly, for portrait sittings, or to attend meetings at the Tate or National Portrait Gallery, of both of which he was a trustee. The 'gaudy and ambitious picture of a don from Durham', to which he refers in his letter, was of Sir James Duff, the retiring Vice-Chancellor of Durham University. In the 1950s Henry was out of fashion as an artist, and he earned his bread-and-butter, or paid for his daughters' school fees, from commissioned retirement portraits of University and other worthies. Most of these are not more than conscientious, but the Duff portrait is one of the best of them. Duff's jazzy academic robes and belligerent expression evoked a response from him, and the portrait (to judge from its photograph) is indeed 'gaudy' – for Henry, at least, the frequently sub-fusc colouring of whose pictures takes some penetration before one realises their quality.

Henry's sitters were sparingly fed with Priory biscuits and glasses of sherry, and were popular if they brought a friend (preferably female) to entertain them, so that Henry did not have to talk. Much of his letter to me is concerned with organizing sittings with the don, myself, and Thomas Pakenham, his three sitters in late 1957. The arrangements were complicated because Henry was suffering in one leg from having been injected with a dirty needle on a French holiday; he was in much pain as a result, and sittings were cancelled in consequence.

On 25 October, after a lot of trouble with the leg, he wrote in some depression: '... we expect Henrietta tonight till Sunday night which will cheer me out of the chronic boredom and lethargy and concentration on food and sleep which has come to envelope me. I am sick of reading, and of crossword puzzles, and of music-starvation.' On an earlier and perhaps less successful visit: 'Henrietta blew in with a chap from Coker (?) called Schuldren (?) of the animated sort' [Henry's question marks]. The phrase 'of the animated sort' vividly brings Henry back to me, down to his tone of voice.

In 1960 Henry had a stroke (I think it was a stroke) and was in hospital in Salisbury. I went to see him, and took him for a drive in my car. But he was barely speaking, and it was a depressing occasion. He died not long after. I went with Thomas to the funeral at Coombe Bissett. In addition to the family David Cecil was there, and Leslie Hartley, and Augustus and Dorelia John. I have an image of the two Johns, he ponderous and coat-enveloped, walking very slowly up the path to the church porch – the only time I ever saw either of them. I don't remember them coming to the house afterwards.

I frequently pass the church and graveyard at Coombe Bissett, driving along the A354 to visit friends in Dorset, and say to myself that one of these days I must stop and visit his grave. But graves do not mean all that much to me, and I have never yet done so.

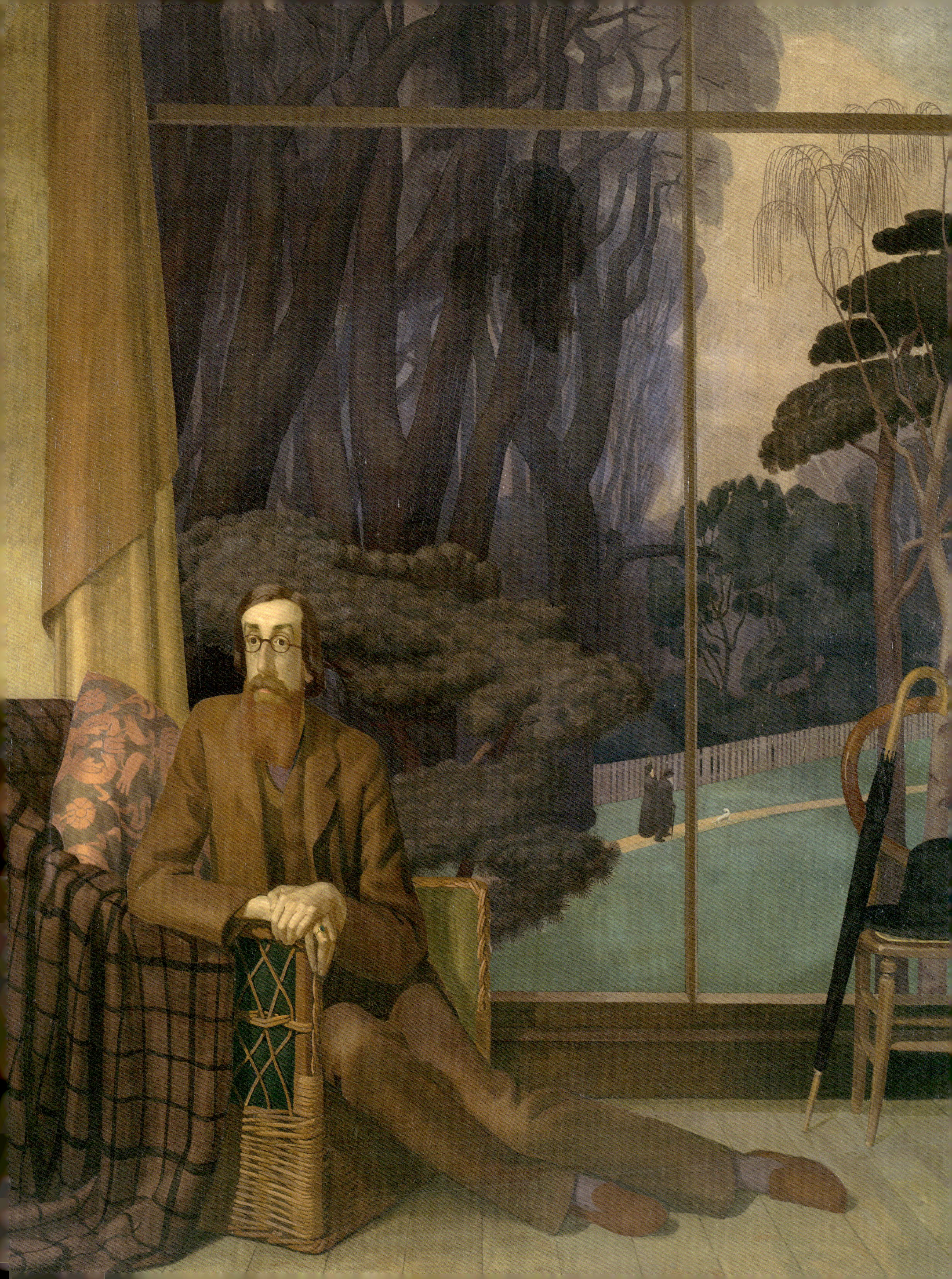

Introduction

HARRY MOORE-GWYN

IN WHAT IS PROBABLY HENRY LAMB'S MOST FAMOUS painting, its awkward sitter, his friend the writer and critic Lytton Strachey, is strangely pushed to the picture's lower left-hand corner, the rest of the monumental canvas dwarfing him from above (fig. 1). Over him stands the large window of the artist's then studio at the Vale of Health Hotel on Hampstead Heath with the dark shadowy trees occupying the larger central section of the canvas. To the right, against a chair on which sits Strachey's distinctive hat, leans his umbrella. Full of brilliantly playful devices, *Portrait of Lytton Strachey* is a portrait in the complete sense, the sitter's languorous personality conveyed not merely through the conventional device of his own figure (a fraction of the work itself) but through the drooping trees beyond, which appear to ape his own portrait, and the elongated awkwardness of the whole composition. The subdued brown-greens of his palette also appear to blend Strachey into his very surroundings. It is typical of Lamb's most memorable works, which characteristically appear at first sight familiar but which on prolonged acquaintance are both sophisticated and unconventional. His Lytton Strachey is a complete character study, worked on through time (in this case through years of friendship). It is arguably the most famous picture of the writer and today forms part of the collection at Tate Britain as one of the gallery's best-known and memorable twentieth-century British portraits.[1] And yet, as has often been observed, how many seeing this work and knowing the sitter would also be able to name the artist?[2]

FIG. 1
Lytton Strachey, 1914
Oil on canvas, 244.5 × 178.4 cm
Tate (Presented by the Trustees of the Chantrey Bequest 1957, T00118)

You could perhaps blame a career that was primarily dedicated to the painting of portraits (among these are great cultural figures of the age such as Strachey, Evelyn Waugh, Benjamin Britten, Anthony Powell and Cecil Beaton) for the fact that Lamb's own particular talents have been at times eclipsed by those of his more widely famous sitters. Also to blame, though, has been Lamb's habit of being notoriously hard to pigeon-hole within the context of a twentieth-century British art establishment that has often been too keen to assign labels. His associations with Strachey, Lady Ottoline Morrell and Duncan Grant (whom he had met in Paris) have often aligned him with the Bloomsbury Group and yet he was always keen to distance himself as much as possible from the style of a movement whose adherents he largely despised. He was a founder member of the Camden Town Group and yet little that he showed at their inaugural exhibitions suggested common ground with its other founder members in either style of execution or subject matter.[3] He was a pupil of Augustus John, but would later strongly distance himself from him, and a mentor to the young Stanley Spencer, even if their interdependence and mutual influence still remains a subject of debate. The exquisitely fine 'Slade' style of his early drawing has regularly led to him being claimed as an alumnus of the institution, although he never attended the Slade School of Art, studying in Chelsea under the tutelage of Augustus John and William Orpen, having abandoned his medical training in Manchester.

Instead, the narrative of early twentieth-century British painting has tended to cast Lamb as an outsider. Although constantly referred to in the indexes of work on John, Spencer and the Bloomsbury Group, he remains one of only a handful of British artists of his calibre to have had no significant recent monograph devoted to him nor a substantial retrospective of his work within the last

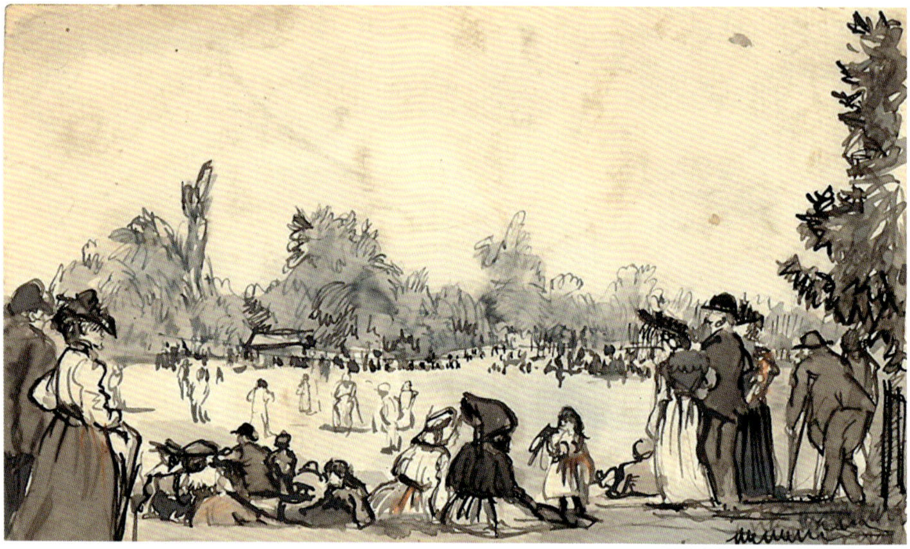

FIG. 2
A day in the park, c.1905
Wash over pen and ink on paper, 99 × 170 mm
The Henry Lamb Estate

thirty years.[4] Lamb also worked for the last few decades of his life as a highly in-demand painter of portraits. This existence provided him with a steady flow of commissions but the work varied widely in quality, frequently lacking the ability to engage with the viewer beyond the confines of the institution or family it was painted for.

Although Lamb was born in Adelaide in Australia, his family soon returned to Manchester, and it was this city that would be identified as his hometown and provide the backdrop for the first couple of decades of his life. His father Horace Lamb was a distinguished mathematician and professor at Manchester University, and Lamb went on to study at Manchester Grammar School before gaining a place at medical school in the university. If Manchester would in time hold an ambiguous place in both the artistic and personal life of the artist, it also proved a source for some significant early influences. Two artists there would provide crucial early encouragement, Joseph Knight (1837–1909), his teacher at Manchester Grammar School, and Francis Dodd (1874–1949), one of the first figures to recognize Lamb's talents and even find him willing buyers. Another influence appears to be Manchester Art Gallery, where he had admired the murals by the Pre-Raphaelite painter Ford Maddox Brown, and would have absorbed the museum's extensive collection of earlier European paintings. Later, when in correspondence with the gallery's then curator Lawrence Haward over the inclusion of his war painting *Advance Dressing Station on the Struma* in the gallery's collection, he even spoke of how he had been touched by that museum's very atmosphere: 'I wonder what room will honour it. I have a great many strong though a bit vague feelings about that Gallery which I suppose I have spent more (certainly more impressionable) hours in than any other: and I was thinking about it a good deal while composing that rather melancholy scheme of colours.'[5]

Some of his surviving artworks from this very earliest period offer a few clues to his later work: cartoons for the *Manchester Medical Student's Gazette* of 1904 show a swift natural sense of line – an illustrator's ability which is evident in his sketchbooks throughout his life and is also apparent in his late subject paintings. Other, topographical, drawings, including an early study of a park scene (fig. 2) and a pencil drawing of Westminster Hall probably executed soon after Lamb's arrival in London in 1905,[6] are technically accurate pieces of almost architectural draughtsmanship. They strongly recall the precise drawings and etchings of his mentor Dodd as well as the printmaker and artist Sir Muirhead Bone. Yet there were also early hints at his abilities as a portraitist and there exist competent portrait drawings in chalks on buff paper (in the collection of the artist's family) signed and dated to as early as 1903.[7] Although still hesitant in execution, they employ a technique, combining red, white and black chalk, that would remain characteristic of the studies for larger commissions he made throughout his career. In 1904 he would go on to execute a dapper self-portrait in a competent late Edwardian style, the artist shown facing right in a black hat.[8]

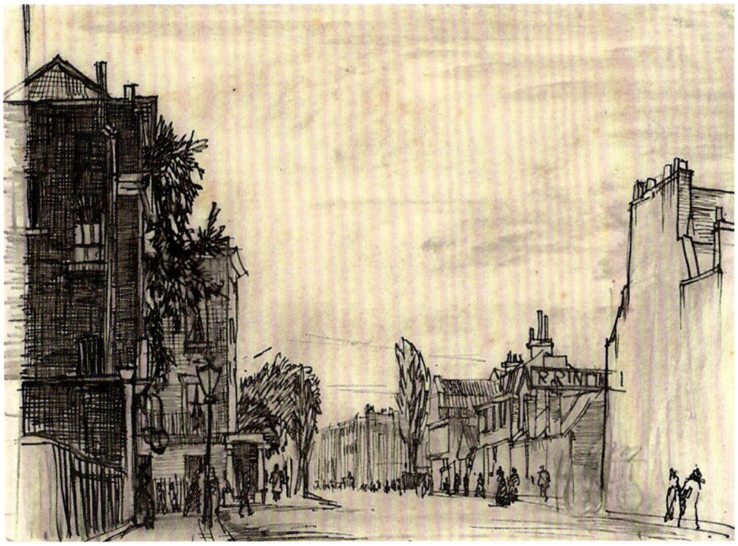

FIG. 3
Scene on a high street, c.1905 (detail)
Wash over pen and ink on paper,
160 × 184 mm
The Henry Lamb Estate

Lamb would soon abandon medicine and Manchester and (with the support and encouragement of Dodd) came to London in July 1905. In January 1906 he enrolled at the Chelsea School of Art, founded by the two towering young figures from Lamb's generation at the Slade, Augustus John and William Orpen. Lamb, six years younger than John, quickly fell under the elder artist's influence, not merely in his work (his drawing from the period can be said to match and even surpass that of his master), but also in his appearance – his confident, Bohemian self-portraits from 1906 showing him cultivating a beard and wearing an earring.

Lamb's bond with John would extend far beyond artistic style into the deeper ties of his personal life. He would soon seek to distance himself stylistically from John, even if his shadow lurked in the background of much of Lamb's pre-War work. A more personal bond came in the form of Lamb's first wife, the wild and enigmatic Nina Forrest, who the artist had met at Manchester in 1905. She was soon renamed Euphemia by Lamb, a reference to her perceived resemblance to a painting of St Euphemia by one of his favourite artists, Andrea Mantegna.[9] Although Lamb and Euphemia's marriage would prove a brief affair (despite the fact they would not actually divorce until 1928), she would soon become one of John's favourite models and part of his close circle. Letters from Augustus John to Lamb whilst Lamb was studying in Paris suggest that John would be an important source of information for him on the affairs of the constantly wandering Euphemia: 'I know nothing of Euphemia's doings I regret. I trust she has not taken herself out of sight.'[10] At around the same time Lamb would develop a love for John's muse and partner Dorelia McNeill that would last well into the 1920s (see fig. 4).

Having been sucked into the John circle, Lamb would relatively swiftly choose to distance himself from it, perhaps because of John's treatment of Dorelia (and possibly in a vain hope that she might leave John for him) but conceivably also on account of his identification with John within the circles of contemporary art criticism. Much of Lamb's work in the years before he travelled to Brittany in 1910 owes a debt to John, not just in his drawings, which at times can almost be mistaken for John's, but also in his choice of female sitters (Dorelia's sister Edie McNeill was the subject of several of his best early portraits) and in the more painterly style of his oil paintings. Early reviews, including from the critic P.G. Konnody, clearly no admirer of Lamb, were quick to dismiss him as an imitator: 'Unfortunately, it is not this phase of Mr John's art[11] that seems to attract imitators, but the extravagance of his more 'advanced' style .... Mr Henry Lamb seems to be deadly serious in his emulation of all that is disconcerting in Mr John, and the results are truly deplorable.'[12] A few years later (in April 1913) when writing to Strachey on the subject of the Contemporary Art Society (CAS) show at the Goupil Gallery, Lamb would dismiss one of John's most iconic portraits, a work of which in the previous decade he would have probably declared himself a fervent admirer: 'The CAS show ... is a depressing show .... Le Grand Maitre himself is

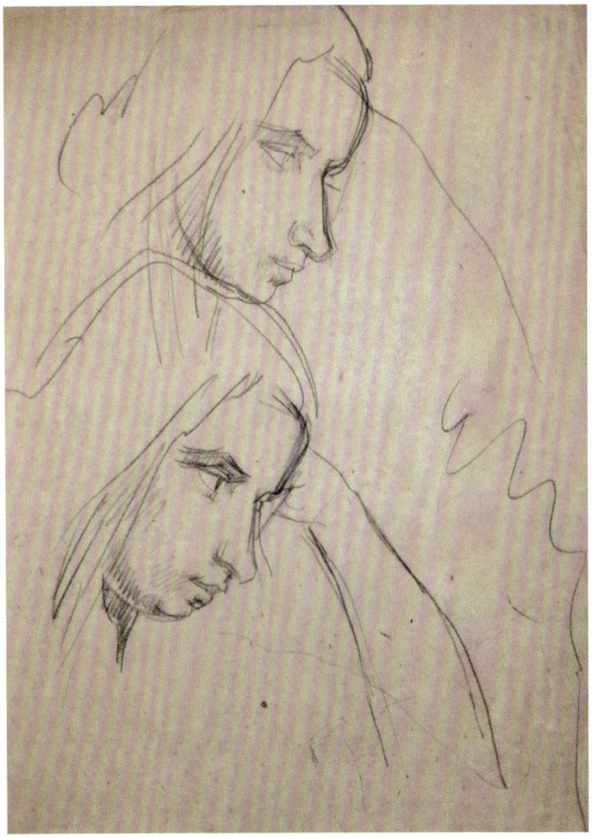

FIG. 4
Studies of Dorelia (detail)
Pencil on paper, 360 × 240 mm
The Henry Lamb Estate

horribly represented by that damned picture of Dorelia smiling.'[13] Lamb would forever owe a debt to John for his transformation from the workmanlike draughtsman and portraitist of 1905 to the bold and self-assured painter he had become, but to fight against the criticism of imitation he would be forced to forge a new direction. To achieve this he would need to displace himself from the small chattering world of critical London to the wide open vistas of the primitive Brittany of 1910.

It was John who had provided Lamb with the initial encouragement he needed to visit France and to continue his artistic training in 1907 at the L'Ecole de la Palette in Montparnasse. At around this time Lamb also made regular excursions outside Paris, including to Brittany in 1907 and to Normandy with the John family in 1908. Although details of some of these trips remain sketchy, it can be supposed that it is here that he may have had some indirect or even direct contact with some key figures in the modern art scene. It is known that John visited Picasso's studio and the two men's correspondence suggests that John introduced him to the young Spanish painter's work (inducing an enthusiastic response from Lamb).[14] Nor was Lamb lacking in curiosity or proactivity in searching out cutting-edge art himself. There is a tantalizing comment in a letter from John revealing that he may even have introduced his teacher to the work of Vincent Van Gogh: '... who is this Van Gogh you speak of? It is surprising to find men in England apparently alive to the tendency of modern art to symbolism.'[15] Another artist who was being shown in Paris in 1907 was Paul Gauguin (who had died in 1903). Gauguin had spent the summer of 1886 in the artist's colony at Pont Aven on the Brittany coast and he returned periodically during the following years, helping to the forge the more modern brand of illustrative Symbolism that signified a break with the Impressionists and the more restrained Symbolism of artists such as Pierre Puvis de Chavannes. So strong were Gauguin's associations with Pont Aven by 1910 that it was easy to forget that the French harbour town and its surroundings had drawn in artists since at least the 1850s, amongst them the American painters Robert Wylie and Frederick Bridgeman and the influential French Orientalist painter Jean-Léon Gérôme. Like many artists before him Lamb had probably also been drawn to the cheap standard of living that this stretch of the Brittany coast offered to the struggling artist, as well as its attractive location, cut off on a limb from the mechanization and modernization seen elsewhere in modern France. Another less acknowledged source for his attraction to the area may come from further back in Lamb's artistic journey. His first teacher, Joseph Knight, had been a founder of the Manchester School of Painters, a progressive group of artists from the area which rebelled against traditional techniques in art schools of the era. One element of this included an interest in French-style *plein-air* painting techniques, and a number of the group spent time working in Pont Aven for a period of months as early as the 1870s. It is very unlikely that Lamb would not have been at least aware of the region during his time spent under Knight's wing.

It has previously been supposed that Lamb first alighted on Doëlan, the small fishing port a few miles along the coast from Pont Aven, in 1910, but letters to Lamb from John in the summer and early autumn of 1907 show that he was staying in the port back then and already sharing his experiences of Brittany with his teacher.[16] Brittany's people, places and customs had thus had some three years to ferment in Lamb's imagination before he was to return there on one of his most formative trips in 1910. Here he found lodgings with the Favennec family, a large clan of a husband and wife with some twelve children who would provide genuine friendship as well as models for some of the artist's most engaging early mature works. Working in Doëlan in the summer of 1910 and summer and spring of 1911 Lamb filled sketchbooks with studies ranging from highly detailed ink drawings of the rocky coastline, studies of the heads of the Favennec family and ideas for more advanced compositions (see, for example, cat. nos. 3, 5, 7 and 8). His most successful early paintings from the period were small *plein-air* panel paintings such as *Breton Boy* (fig. 5) and *Breton Cowherd* (private collection) – atmospheric, dappled, slightly Gauguinesque landscapes with figures that show the clear influence of the vibrant oil sketches that Augustus John was executing of his family at around the same date. But the greatest pictures from the period were more worked reflections on his experiences there. The two most significant works in this vein were his *Death of a Peasant* from 1911 (cat. 4) and *Lamentation* (see cat. 51), both subjects a heartfelt response to the death of Madame Favennec, the family's matriarch – an event Lamb himself had witnessed on his first trip to Doëlan in 1910.

It would be wrong either to ignore or to overstate the influence of Gauguin on Lamb at this date. A review by Frank Rutter of Lamb's contributions to the first Camden Town Exhibition in 1911 astutely observed that Lamb was 'a modern classicist just as Gauguin – whom he so discriminately admires'.[17] This perceived selectivity in his admiration of Gauguin's work gets to the heart of Lamb – an artist who abhorred the idea of being swept up by any movement or the assumed discipleship of any artist. Indeed, following a more lukewarm response to Gauguin's work at the seminal Post-Impressionist Exhibition in London in the following year, Lamb was moved to write: 'Thanks to my disillusionment about Gauguin at ... [the] exhibition ... I need no longer hold out my left hand to these French models except in as far as sketching from nature goes'.[18] Lamb had been true to his word, for whilst works like the startling head-on portrait *Breton Youth* (cat. 3) owes a clear debt to the French artist, the majority of his most important works from the time, such as *Death of a Peasant* and *Lamentation,* were retrospective pieces, responses over time, through work in the studio, to that emotionally charged event in the previous year. Indeed, for *Death of a Peasant*, perhaps his greatest Breton work, Lamb looked not to Post-Impressionism but to his long-held admiration for the Old Masters, including Andrea Mantegna and painters of the Northern European Renaissance.

Meanwhile, across the channel, Lamb seemed scarcely aware of his place as a select member of one of twentieth-century British art's most important movements. Although the Camden Town Group would prove relatively short-lived and hold only three exhibitions, in 1911 and 1912, the light it cast on contemporary urban life and its sophisticated engagement with modern European art of the period would have a lasting influence on art of the following decades, including that associated with the London Group which developed out of it in 1913. Lamb's entrée to the group had come through its most charismatic leading light, Walter Sickert, who had been an enthusiastic early admirer of Lamb's work, even hawking his paintings to potential buyers at his influential Fitzroy Street meetings. Lamb was one of sixteen founder members and his submissions, mainly of the work he had produced in Brittany, were at odds with the more cosmopolitan, London-centred works of his colleagues. His correspondence from Donegal suggests that he used a fellow member, James Bolivar Manson, as his envoy for the final Camden Town show, engaging with him only to record logistical elements of the dispatching, pricing and titling of the works he had submitted and seeming largely uninterested in the workings of the group itself.[19] Despite this, and perhaps because of some of his obvious stylistic differences with other members of the group, his work received some favourable reviews. His *Portrait of Edie McNeill: Red and Gold* (private collection), exhibited at the Carfax Gallery at the second Camden Town Exhibition in December 1911, was described as 'an admirably firm and well characterised study',[20] while *The Evening Standard and St James's Gazette* declared: 'The honours of the exhibition go to Mr Henry Lamb for his portrait ... this head and shoulders of a girl in red has the strange dignity and beauty that come from painting what is felt rather than seen'.[21] Perhaps more telling, though, in view of the direction that Lamb's work would take, was the reception that he received for the arguably more flawed full-length portrait of Edie McNeill he painted on an empty cliff edge in Brittany (cat. 9). This work was exhibited just prior to the second Camden Town Exhibition at the New English

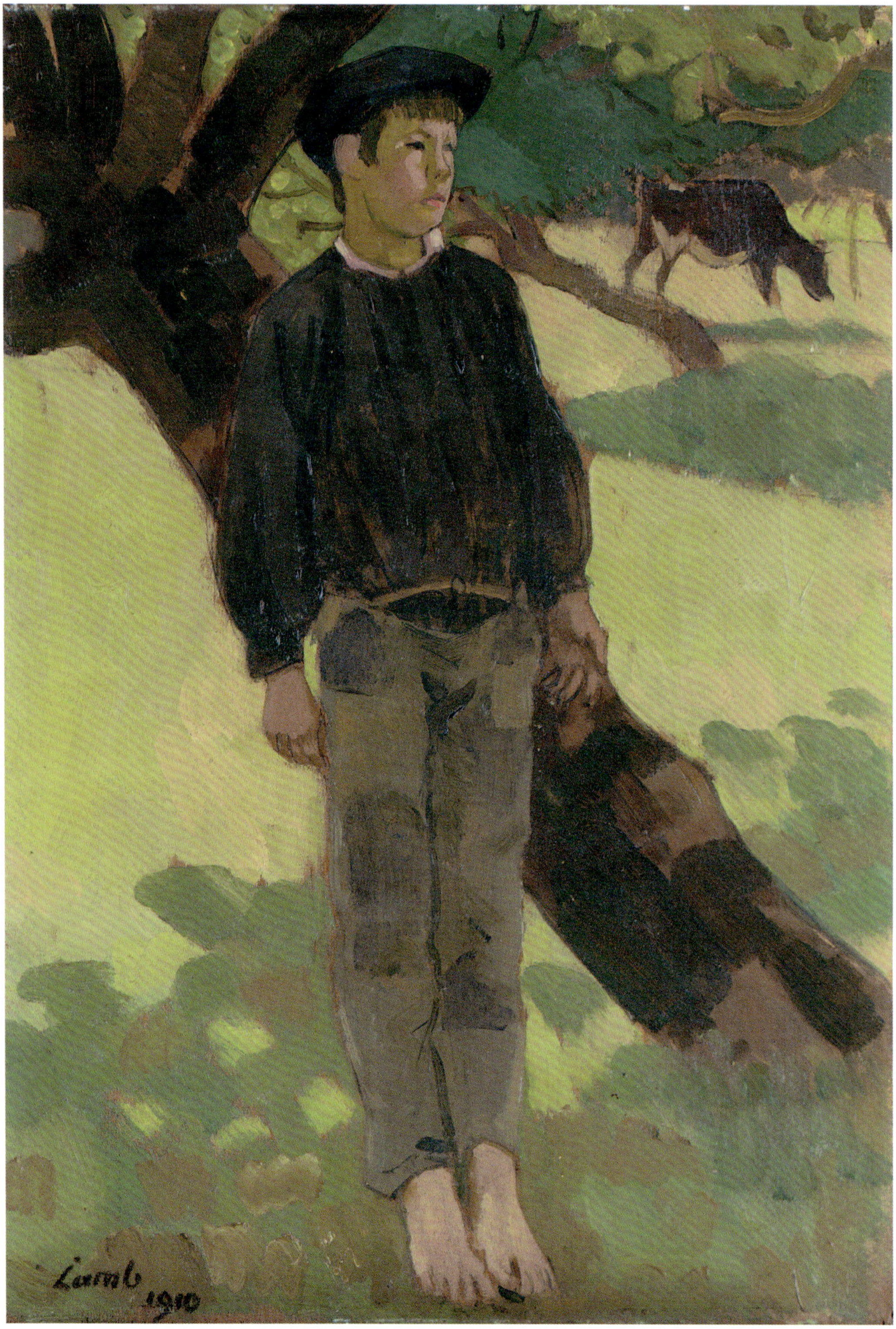

FIG. 5
Breton Boy, 1910
Oil on panel, 35.5 × 25.5 cm
Private collection

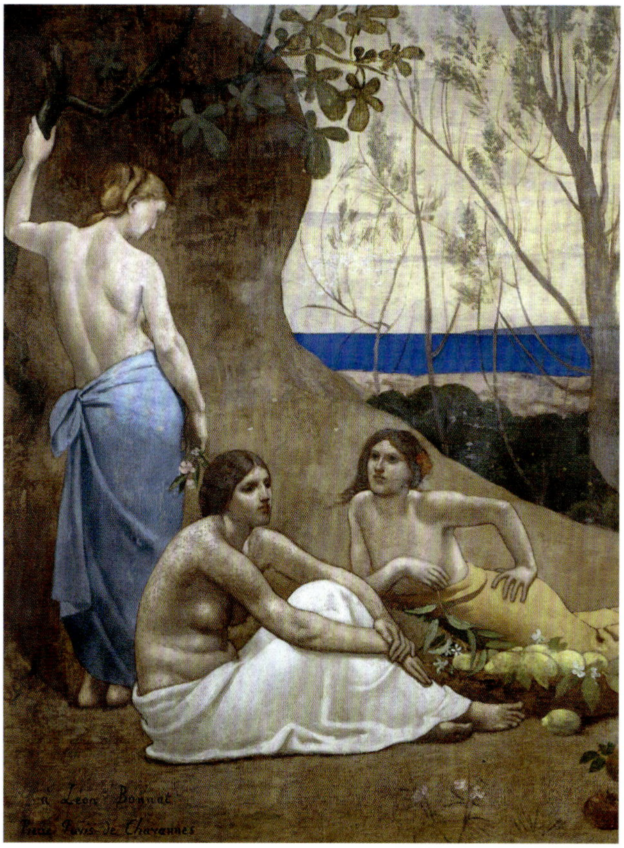

FIG. 6
PUVIS DE CHAVANNES
The Happy Land (*Doux Pays*), exhibited 1882 (detail)
Oil on canvas, 230 × 300 cm (whole)
Musée Bonnat, Bayonne, France

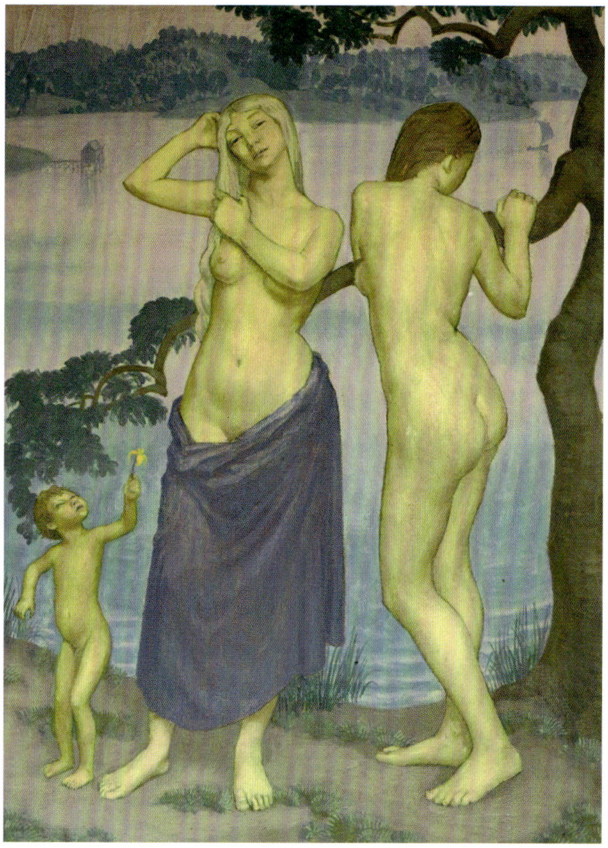

FIG. 7
The Lake, 1911
Tempera on canvas, 61 × 45.7 cm
Jonathan Clark Fine Art

Art Club in November 1911. *The Glasgow Herald* critic declared it 'an exquisite and subtle harmony of greys, the only touch of colour in the picture being the narrow strip of red that border's the girl's neck',[22] and that of *Bazaar* exclaimed: 'How supple the plainly clad figure, and how well its lines fill the unbroken background'.[23] In spite of Lamb's love-hate relationship with critical circles in pre-War London, such positive reviews can hardly have failed to make an impression and one that could only encourage the more individual direction his work would soon take.

In the years between 1910 and the outbreak of the First World War, Lamb's work can appear to meander through European styles from Augustus John to Gauguin, from Puvis de Chavannes in *The Lake* (see figs. 6 and 7) to Picasso's 'Blue Period' in *Phantasy* (cat. 10). This period, however, also accounts for the majority of the artist's most defining paintings. His early attempts to forge what would become his own style of English classicism, guided by these influences but not imitative of them, had begun in France not merely through his great successes (*Death of a Peasant* and *Breton Youth*) but also through his relative failures like the large portrait of Edie McNeill (1911) discussed above. More recent critics have tended to focus on this work's imperfections – its unsatisfyingly empty background and the awkward pose of his unengaged sitter.[24] But it is also evidence of a tightening of Lamb's painting technique and a nod towards the subtle, sometimes awkward, stylization perceivable not just in his great Gola Island paintings in 1912–13 but also in the inspired contrivance of his Great War works and his portrait groups early in the following decade.

As a painter Lamb had, too, honed his palette, one now permeated by earthy raw umbers and greens, both subdued and subtle and a world away from the vibrant colouring of his contemporaries in the Bloomsbury Group. This he had done at the risk of unfavourable coverage from the prevailing critical opinion, even if, as in the case of Desmond McCarthy writing in *Eye Witness* in 1911, his evident talents would still show through: 'There is something dour in his art; the clayey greens, of which he is so fond, is [sic] not in itself a pleasing colour, yet his pictures have a charm that lasts.'[25] At the same time Lamb would become increasingly well-connected. A passionate relationship with the influential socialite Lady Ottoline Morrell, whose home at Garsington Manor would prove a magnet for cultural figures both near and far, introduced him to a wider circle that would include the Bloomsbury Group, Dora Carrington and the philosopher Bertrand Russell.

Lamb had been in England for well under a year after his second Breton trip when his friend George Kennedy suggested a visit to the northern Irish coast of Donegal. Kennedy, whom he had met in Paris in 1906 and who following the War established himself as an architect, was a key friend in the early part of the artist's life. As well as becoming the central subject in one of the artist's most successful family portraits in 1921 (cat. 30), Kennedy was also one of only a few admirers of his work to whom Lamb would (at least on occasion) listen. He was also the writer of the first monograph on Lamb, published by Ernest Benn in 1924. Perhaps most importantly it was through Kennedy that Lamb would meet his second wife, Lady Pansy Pakenham, at the end of the 1920s. On his arrival in Ireland Lamb established himself in Middletown, a few miles from Kennedy's house at Gortahork. The work resulting from his Irish trips includes some of the artist's most beautiful drawings, frequently head studies of Irish men and women on the mainland and afterwards on the remote island of Gola. In time some of these would be built up and integrated through study after study, in the manner of a Renaissance painter in his studio, to one of his most compelling and complex compositions, *Fisherfolk, Gola Island* of 1913 (cat. 11).

Fisherfolk has a significant place in lyric late Romantic painting of the pre-War years. Whilst it can be seen in the context of some of John's larger figure compositions, like his *Lyric Fantasy* of the following year, its similarities to John are largely superficial. It is a world away from such works in execution and arguably far more successful in construction. Whilst Lamb's composition certainly adopts elements of style from a myriad of sources – from the French Symbolist Maurice Denis to the quirky arrangements of figures in Stanley Spencer's *Apple Gatherers* (fig. 8), which he had recently seen for the first time, to perhaps a trace of Pre-Raphaelitism – the end result is emphatically his own. Intriguingly, Lamb's correspondence from the period 1911–14 dwells very little on his actual practice as a painter. It instead reveals an artist of wide-ranging cultural interests, from Dostoyevsky to Plato, from Bach and Beethoven to Busoni. He would later refer to *Fisherfolk* as his 'Gola Sonata',[26] a conscious reference to the work's satisfying harmony and synthesis at a time when music was as much (if not more) on his mind as art.

A notable characteristic of Lamb's personality was an apparently unegotistical ability both to voice admiration for painters who inspired him and to help and defend them when a fight was needed. In the summer of 1912 he had been co-opted to run a petition against the French government for their heavy-handed reaction to the Oscar Wilde tomb by the American British sculptor Jacob Epstein, which was soon to be installed at the Père Lachaise Cemetery. Elsewhere (rather as Francis Dodd had done for him), he was keen to support and acquire works by fellow artists, particularly if it meant getting the better of art dealers, a breed he generally detested. In his final home at Coombe Bissett in Wiltshire, Lamb's daughter Felicia Palmer recalls how the walls were hung not with his own paintings but with examples of work by artists, young and old, who he had helped and encouraged, amongst them Stanley and Gilbert Spencer, Henry Moore and Raymond Coxon.[27] No artist did he support more than the young Stanley Spencer. Hugely taken by Spencer's Slade School prize-winning painting *The Apple Gatherers,* he was infuriated with the Contemporary Art Society (where Clive Bell was one of the buyers) for their refusal to recognize its genius. He conceived of a scheme by which he bought the work, with the intention of selling it on to a collector at no profit to himself: it was eventually bought by Edward Marsh. Despite the amusement Lamb gained from such schemes, in this case getting the better of Bell, one of his least favourite Bloomsbury-ites, it also showed a marked generosity. It was the beginning of a sometimes awkward friendship with Spencer which would be central to his work in the latter part of the 1910s and 1920s, a meeting of minds that would involve a shared interest in art of the Italian

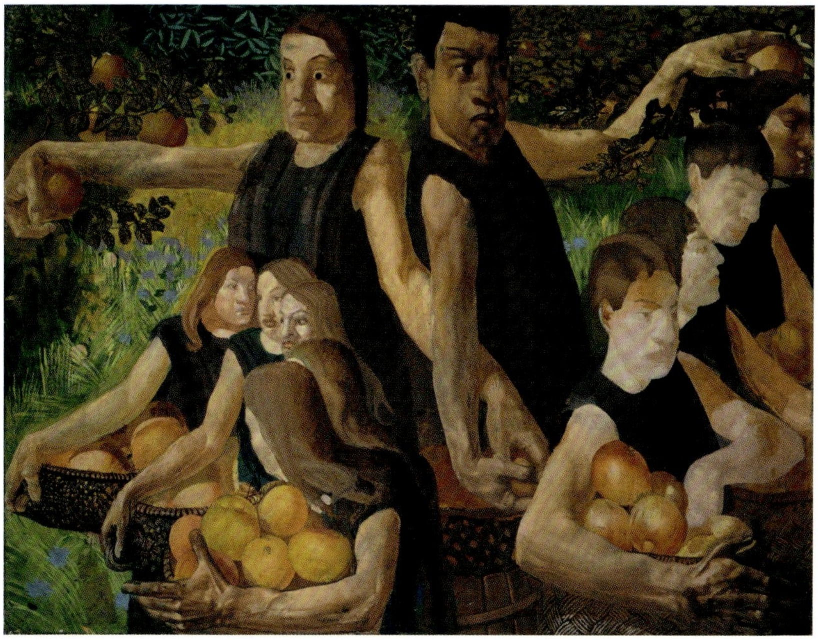

FIG. 8
STANLEY SPENCER
The Apple Gatherers, 1912–13
Oil on canvas, 71.4 × 92.4 cm
Tate (Presented by Sir Edward Marsh 1946, N05663)

Quattrocento and Classical music. It would also involve a two-way sharing of artistic ideas in which Lamb's side of the partnership has perhaps too rarely been given real credit.

In Spencer's long correspondence with Lamb there is much evidence of the way these interests were shared. Rarely, though, in Spencer's constantly self-referential replies to Lamb is the younger artist prepared to utter praise for the elder's work or even talk about it. Instead, Spencer would use Lamb as a sounding board for his anxieties and creative angst, regularly illustrating the letters with sketches of his compositions, and it is hardly surprising if a little of this did not rub off on to Lamb. What also emerges is not merely Lamb's artistic generosity, sharing postcards and books on his favourite Old Masters and playing the piano for Spencer on visits to Cookham, but also his financial generosity, perpetually sending money to the poorer, younger artist. As a cultural guide Lamb would prove invaluable, introducing to Spencer and helping Spencer to cultivate interest in the very Renaissance artists who would provide him with the most enduring inspiration: 'Lorenzetti seems not finer than Giotto ... they are very different. Is Masaccio a Sienese man too? And also Masolino da Panicale? They ... have feelings that Giotto and the rest of his time never had.'[28] On the eve of the First World War, both artists would complete direct and supremely confident self-portraits, perhaps the ultimate evidence of two careers mapping a similar trajectory and announcing their arrival to the art world at around the same time.

A return to medical training at Guy's Hospital and subsequent postings as a medical officer with the Royal Army Medical Corps, first to the Hospital Anglais du Casino in Fécamp in Normandy and later to Salonika and Palestine, would effectively remove any possibility of Lamb practising as an artist until the end of the War. Almost anything that survived did so in a series of miniature sketchbooks, the only artistic materials that were practical enough for his postings abroad. His natural inclination towards portraiture initially continued unabated, his Fécamp sketchbooks showing sensitive head studies of nurses, fellow officers and convalescing soldiers. Once in Palestine his focus appears to shift away from the human element and he made beautifully crafted sketches of the region's dramatic, rocky landscape and distinctive fauna. Nothing in them suggested a wish to engage with the action or showed any intimation of the great large-subject paintings that would be completed at the end of the war.

Lamb had been put forward as a war artist by Francis Dodd in January 1918, but, despite interventions from both Dodd and Muirhead Bone, he was not released from official duty in time to prevent him from being badly gassed only days before the Armistice. Instead

Lamb would produce his final masterpiece of the decade, *Irish Troops in the Judaean Hills Surprised by a Turkish Bombardment* (cat. 14), only subsequently, in 1919, looking back at chilling events of the year before, one of the most impressive contributions to the ultimately unrealised Hall of Remembrance that was proposed following the Armistice in 1918. The Hall of Remembrance was an ambitious scheme of commissions from the British War Memorials Committee of the Ministry of Information. The stated intention had been to depict 'fighting subjects, home subjects and the war at sea and in the air', with a selection of key imposing pictures that would be based on the dimensions of Paolo Uccello's monumental triptych *Battle of San Romano* in the National Gallery, London (c.1435–60). Ultimately the Hall of Remembrance was never built but the paintings that would result from the commission were an inspiring combination of grand history paintings by established artists of the day, amongst them John Singer Sargent, Sir William Orpen and Sir George Clausen, alongside work from the most promising emerging talents, such as C. R.W. Nevinson, Paul and John Nash and Percy Wyndham Lewis. The scheme would do much to help establish the careers of many members of this latter group. Although tantalizingly little correspondence exists between Spencer and Lamb, in 1919 there were striking similarities between the two works the artists submitted to the scheme – Spencer's *Travoys arriving with Wounded at a Dressing Station at Smol, Macedonia, September 1916* and Lamb's *Irish Troops*. Despite these compositional similarities – the horizon of each picture being pushed beyond the upper edge of the canvas and the flattened plane of each subject's viewpoint partly creating a bird's-eye view from above – the impact of the pictures varies. In Spencer's *Travoys* we are suspended above as distant witnesses to the humanitarian work of the army medics, for Lamb the close quarters of the action and steep flattened landscape create an almost claustrophobic effect and a sense of being in the midst of a terrifying event.

Another of the artist's monumental masterpieces also derived from his experiences of the war – *Advance Dressing Station on the Struma* (Manchester Art Gallery), a work directly based on his time as a medical officer in Salonika in 1916. In *Irish Troops* Lamb had self-consciously made a direct reference to the scheme's first inspiration, Uccello's *Battle of San Romano*. In *Advance Dressing Station,* too, Lamb made no attempt to disguise his sources in early European art – the central figure of the cradled wounded soldier being a direct reference to countless depictions of the Pietà (the Virgin holding the lifeless body of the crucified Christ).

As was the case following his other returns from exile, in Brittany and Donegal, Lamb struggled to settle into London life in the years after his discharge from active duty. He went out of his way to spend time away from the city, and as well as a prolonged period painting in Stourpaine in 1921 (where he completed most of the work on *Advance Dressing Station*) he was also a visitor to the John family at Alderney Manor in Dorset. Such associations helped him to alight on Poole, the harbour town where in 1922 he acquired his first house, 10 Hill Street, in amongst the harbour's narrow streets and walkways. Lamb's many attempts at landscape painting were generally conventional and run-of-the-mill. In contrast, the townscape of Poole would prove a rich source for some of his most significant non-figure-based works and he executed a charming and inventive series of paintings based around the rooftops of the town, views down its alleyways and from the back of his home. Here he was able to bring to bear the inventive use of flattened, slanted perspective and subtle stylization that he had just realised in *Irish Troops.* Nowhere is this more true than in one of his earliest street scenes, *Dear Hay Lane, Poole* (1922),[29] the crowds below scattered across the narrow street rather in the manner of his Irish troops darting away from their bombardment. Elsewhere the stage-set forms frame his subjects, as in *Paradise Street* (cat. 23), almost in the manner of the theatrical street scenes of James Pryde. And in a nod to his Camden Town roots he elsewhere appears to observe the harbour unnoticed, much in the way that Sickert did the streets of his Dieppe.

Perhaps more important than his diversions into the street scenes of 1920s Poole was the work he was simultaneously achieving in portraiture and more particularly his group portraits. His self-consciously artificial piecing together of these family groups and conversation pieces can be traced back to the example he had set himself in *Fisherfolk* a decade earlier. And what on first sight can seem like awkwardness and imbalance, in a work like *A Bristol Committee* (1921), would in time become one of the defining elements of his style. This style would reach its climax in the portrait groups *The Anrep Family*

(1920; Museum of Fine Arts, Boston) and *The Kennedy Family* (1921; cat. 30). As with so many of Lamb's most successful portraits, both works depict the families of important friends in the artist's early life – the mosaicist Boris Anrep and the architect George Kennedy. In their constant working through sensitive portrait studies in pencil and smaller preparatory watercolour studies (a technique regularly seen in the building of his larger compositions), he was able to create a tightly rendered and deliberately artificial type of portrait that would anticipate the work of Stanley Spencer a decade later. These works might arguably be regarded as some of his most original contributions to British art. Another highly unconventional conversation piece is the large painting *The Tea Party* (1926; cat. 27). Painted in his dining room at Hill Street, with the Poole gardens stretching out from the bay window beyond, Lamb observes a teatime gathering, Stanley Spencer waxing lyrical at one end of a distended table of exaggerated and elongated proportions. A possible influence on this work may be seen in *Gathering on the Terrace at 47, Downshire Hill, Hampstead* (1925) by his friend Richard Carline, in which Lamb, too, is depicted in a strangely convoluted portrait group which likewise sets the figure of Stanley Spencer out on a limb. But Lamb's composition is more worked and perhaps more emotionally layered – Lamb himself, increasingly lonely during his Poole years, tellingly cast out to the lower edge of the picture with his back to us.

By the late 1920s and apparently coinciding with his meeting his second wife, Lady Pansy Pakenham, Lamb's painting style would notably loosen. Soon gone would be the almost Renaissance tightness in composition and execution seen in *The Kennedy Family,* and in its place a more painterly, apparently spontaneous means of representing a sitter. If the results of this are in some instances more mixed there are, nevertheless, some fine and stylish portraits from the 1920s and 1930s that are redolent of the life of their sitters and the spirit of their age. Notable examples include a suave portrait of Evelyn Waugh (cat. 32), the elegant double portrait of Bryan and Diana Guinness with their wolfhound (cat. 32, of which fig. 9 is a study) and the louche depiction of the young Cecil Beaton seated (1935; private collection). If the results can seem less startling in their originality, Lamb retained an innate ability to create a penetrating and revealing likeness of his sitter and, as pure portraits, many are as successful as those by any comparable British painter

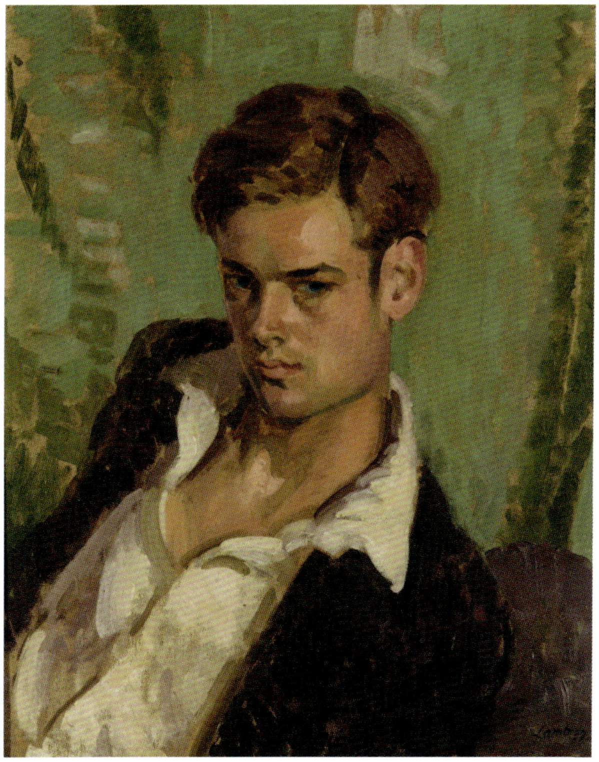

FIG. 9
Bryan Guinness, study for *Lord Moyne with his Parents*, c.1930
Oil on canvas, 69.5 × 58.5 cm
Private collection

of their age. Their spontaneity, too, is perhaps a touch misleading, for, although fresher in their use of paint, the archive of portrait studies with the artist's family suggests that these (in many cases) were built up through careful and accurately executed pencil and chalk portrait studies.

The other major shift in his post-1920s work was marked by a change in his domestic circumstances. Just prior to his marriage to Pansy in 1928, Lamb bought the house that would become the couple's home for the rest of their life, Brookside in Coombe Bissett near Salisbury (fig. 10). The couple's three children followed in the 1930s – Henrietta being born in 1931, Felicia in 1933 and Valentine in 1939. The family life that established itself in the Wiltshire countryside would remain a central focus of the latter part of Lamb's life and his family in particular became a central subject of some of his most successful later portraits and portrait groups. At times they have something of the feel of Stanley Spencer's *Domestic Scenes*, which dwell on that artist's everyday existence with his first wife Hilda Carline, but they are

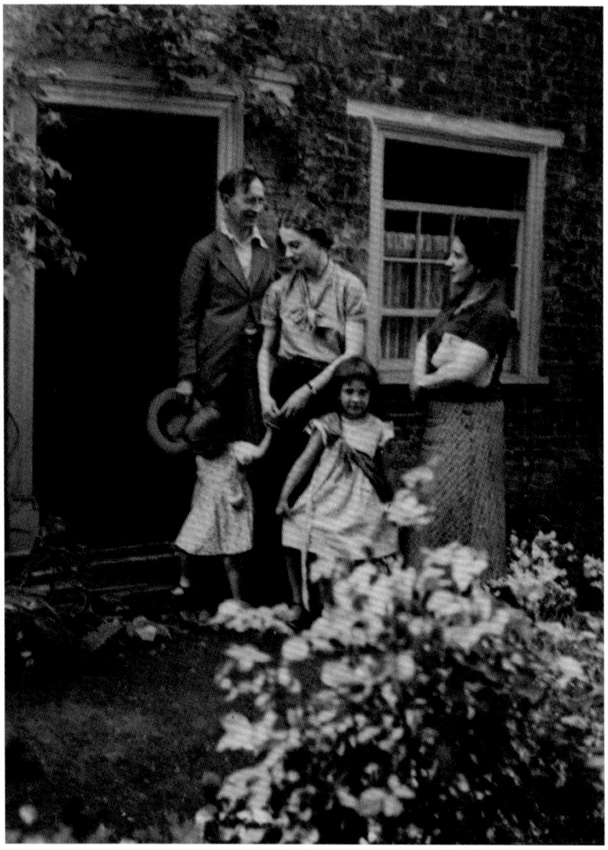

FIG. 10
The Lamb family at 'Brookside', Coombe Bissett, c.late 1930s
The Henry Lamb Estate

more purely naturalistic and only touch on stylization. His use of paint had developed too, focusing on a dappled, impressionistic application of the brush. Lamb's work from this period has been frequently overlooked, but at its best displays a genuine charm as well as his lifelong ability to create a good likeness and reveal the inner soul of his sitters. Amongst these works are *The Artist's Wife* (fig. 11), a delightful and informal portrait of Pansy reading in a chair, and several larger subject pictures including another of Pansy bathing one of their children, *The Infant* (cat. 42), and several surprisingly graphic sketches of Pansy holding their children which, intriguingly, seem to hark back to Augustus John's depictions of Dorelia with her children from c.1907. There are also strong portraits of each of their children, sometimes posed as patient sitters and elsewhere observed from afar playing cards, engaged in children's games, or just resting on the ground (cat. nos. 43, 45, 47, 48).

By the outbreak of the Second World War Lamb found that he had become a reluctant member of the British artistic establishment. He would be elected an Associate of the Royal Academy in 1940 and trusteeships of the National Portrait Gallery and the Tate Gallery would follow in 1942 and 1944. In 1939 he was commissioned by the Friends of Birmingham to paint a portrait of then Prime Minister Neville Chamberlain. In the event the portrait would be slow to progress and was left unfinished at Chamberlain's death in 1940. In the meantime, following the outbreak of war in 1939, the War Artists Advisory Committee (WAAC) had been established under the single-minded direction of Kenneth Clark. Appointed in February 1940, Lamb was one of the earliest painters to be approached to be an official war artist. He was one of only eleven salaried War Artists on the scheme, and his tenure was exceeded only by Edward Ardizzone. Despite this honour he would remain emotionally detached from his role in a war in which (unlike the First World War) his position was to be one of a distant observer to the edge of the sidelines. He somewhat wistfully wrote to the Ministry of Information in 1940: 'I must face the fact that my contact ... is just that of a journalist and the experiences can hardly come from within as they did in my pictures of the other war'.[30] Perhaps confirming the degree to which this effected the end results, Kenneth Clark himself later wrote (perhaps damning with faint praise): 'He was the most reliable of all those who worked for us on the War Artists Advisory Committee'.[31]

Lamb's initial task was portraiture and he made large numbers of portrait drawings of not only the great and the good but also of ordinary servicemen. He also made paintings observing army life on the home front, including engineers working on aeroplanes and of the 40th Tank Battalion on exercises in Ashdown Forest. His most successful wartime partnership was not, however, with the British Army but with Canadian troops – a meeting with their High Commissioner, Vincent Massey, in 1941 leading to his largest body of work, shadowing their 12th Tank Battalion throughout the latter part of that year as they moved from Sussex to the Thames Estuary at Hadleigh. Lamb later wrote to E.M. Dickey (the secretary of the WAAC) in December 1941: 'They are incomparable soldiers – no dead wood – & I wish, I wish ... there were more as good. All ranks.'[32]

The style of these genre works bears a conscious similarity to the work of the illustrator Edward

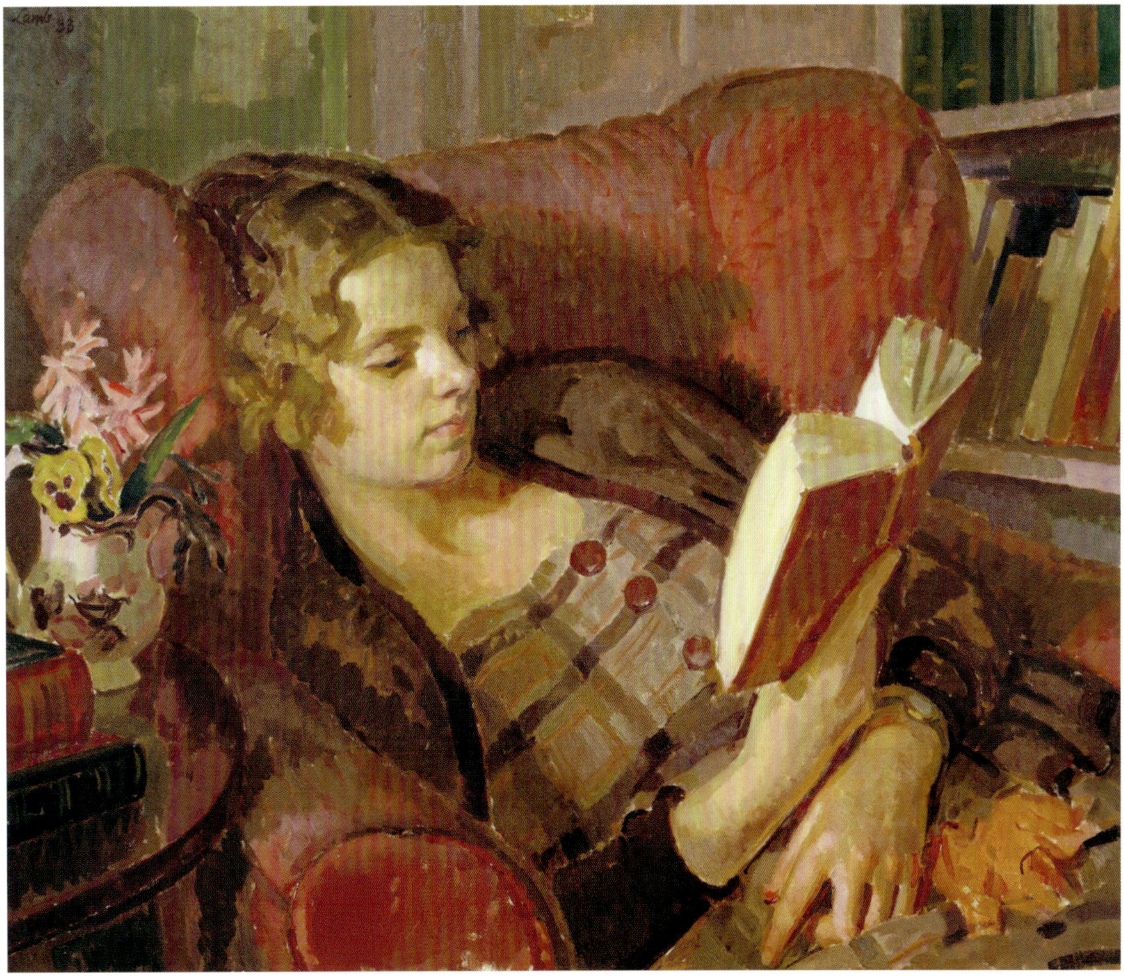

FIG. 11
Henry Lamb
The Artist's Wife, 1933
Oil on canvas, 63.5 × 76.2 cm
Tate (Presented by the Trustees
of the Chantrey Bequest 1934, NO4749)

Ardizzone, whom Lamb had met when he was working near Coombe Bissett in the summer of 1940. He even wrote to the Ministry of Information that his work might be 'something of the sort that Ardizzone has given you though mine would be less humorous and I'm afraid much less stylish'.[33] The results indeed suggest that Lamb's comment was not merely one of modesty. The subjects were generally quirky and swiftly observed scenes from everyday army life – engineers hard at work mending a truck, their feet protruding humorously from the vehicle's undercarriage, the same troops (perhaps) napping on the grass nearby, or queuing at the clothing store in army pay week. As ever spontaneity did not come naturally and, in contrast to the swift on-the-spot execution of Ardizzone's work, Lamb's sketchbooks suggest a characteristic working up of his subjects through constant Biro and pencil drawings and watercolour studies. The artist's daughter Henrietta Phipps regularly referred to the fact that her father never considered himself a natural watercolourist, but his studies for these (and other) works are perhaps fresher and more naturally executed than many of the resulting finished oils.[34] Arguably this was a medium to which he should have dedicated more time.

In the years following the end of the Second World War Lamb continued to send works for exhibition at the

Royal Academy, to which he was elected as a full member in 1949. He also held shows at the Leicester Galleries in 1949 and 1956, and contributed a work, *Nightlife*, to the Festival of Britain exhibition *Sixty Paintings for '51* in 1951. Elsewhere, though, there is evidence that his enthusiasm had waned, and he was at times plagued by depression and a lack of confidence in the success of his work. On the reception of his 1949 Leicester Galleries show, he wrote to Evelyn Waugh: 'Few people will attend nowadays to such a quiet show, no conundrums for the ingenuity of the art critic, no stunts'.[35] In the same letter he observed that the only encouraging comment came from Ardizzone, who praised his show of 'straightforward painting ... like a breath of fresh air'. He showed the same lack of engagement with the modern art scene, and the artist who had noticed Picasso and Van Gogh in Paris in 1907 would praise John Nash and Edward Bawden at one of the National Gallery's war shows in 1941 but fail to pass any comment on the work of Henry Moore and Graham Sutherland in the same exhibition – artists whose vision was unstoppably on the ascendency in mid-1940s Britain.[36]

History has rather unfairly tended to dismiss outright most of Lamb's later work, but some of his finest individual pure portraits come from the 1930s or 1940s. Some of his very late self-portraits, admirably honest insights into his frequently dejected moods, possess a powerful, almost piercing quality. It is, nevertheless, hard to escape the fact that Lamb will be remembered for the art he created either side of the First World War. No decade and a half of British art would be more fruitful than these years – a time of constant evolution unparallelled in its richness of creative talent. Here Lamb made his own particular contribution, sometimes part of and sometimes skirting around the edge of the period's most significant movements and in the immediate circle of some of the era's most important artists. Despite this, at his best he was able to retain a refreshing independence and a stubborn refusal to be pigeon-holed by movements and artistic styles. In 1913, while he painted *Fisherfolk*, the location of his studio, Hampstead Heath, would provide the inspiration for Nevinson and Ethelbert White's zanily futuristic depiction of a bank holiday on the Heath.[37] These works seem miles apart and with this comparison in mind it is hard to view Lamb's as the artistic vision that represents the more prevailing modern direction. Indeed, it may be tempting to view Lamb's poetic strain of classicism as a dead end. To do so, though, would surely be to do it a disservice. Lamb's work had certainly not taken the fashionable direction but, looking ahead to the 1920s, it could perhaps be seen as the heir to the Quattrocento world of the British School of Rome and to artists such as Sir Thomas Monnington and Winifred Knights, figures whose reputations today are enjoying a long overdue reappraisal. It is easy to see, for the same reason, why he has been left out of museum shows on the Camden Town Group but was included in John Christian's show *The Late Romantics* at the Barbican in 1998, an exhibition that highlighted an almost forgotten strain of realism in British painting that continued deep into the twentieth century.[38]

Even in this regard Lamb keeps us guessing. What were his influences as he embarked on *Fisherfolk* – was it French Symbolism, or Stanley Spencer? Or is there even a perceptible nod to Masaccio's *Resurrection of the Son of Theophilus* in the Brancacci Chapel, with the crowded assemblies of portrait groups peering out almost awkwardly from the canvas? Is his *Lytton Strachey* the forging of a new brand of classically influenced modernism or was he the heir to the swagger portraits of Reynolds and Gainsborough (as the introduction to his 1961 memorial show seems to suggest)?[39] Do his Breton peasants reflect the influence of Gauguin or the anguished Northern European tradition of Grünewald? Lamb's letters reveal a complex and highly intelligent mind beyond the surface of the canvas, steeped in European philosophy, classical music and literature. Rarely are his sources as familiar as we first think. They remain open instead to a healthy debate – one that is all too necessary to aid his emergence from the shadows of the more obviously famous circles around him.

NOTES

1 Dora Carrington's 1916 portrait of Strachey (National Portrait Gallery) is at least as well known as Lamb's.
2 For example, 'Briefly Famous', review by Michael McNay of *Henry Lamb, The Artist and his Friends* by Keith Clements, *The Guardian*, 2 May 1985: 'Everyone knows the picture, and everyone that the languid sitter was Lytton Strachey. Only a few people remember the painter was Henry Lamb'.
3 His painting of Lytton Strachey and his celebrated portrait of Leonard Woolf (probably by virtue of the sitter being a Bloomsbury member) have often been claimed as Bloomsbury works and both were included in Richard Shone's *The Art of Bloomsbury*, exh. cat., Tate, 2002. Conversely Lamb was left out of the 2007 Tate show *Modern Painters: The Camden Town Group* and as of December 2017 does not even appear amongst the lengthy list of Camden Town members on the Tate website.
4 Keith Clements's *Henry Lamb, The Artist and his Friends,* Bristol, 1985, is by far the most substantial work on Lamb to date and an invaluable resource for anyone researching the painter. The last major retrospective, at Manchester City Art Gallery (later travelling to Birmingham, Bristol and York), just preceded the book in 1984. Another smaller but notable show on Lamb was held at Charleston, Firle, September–October 2002.
5 Letter from Henry Lamb to Lawrence Haward, 10 August 1921, quoted by Jonathan Meuli, 'Henry Lamb: A Survey of his Life and Works' (B.A. thesis), Cambridge, 1980, p. 2.
6 In the collection of the artist's widow in 1984; see *Henry Lamb (1883–1960),* exh. cat., Manchester Art Gallery, 1984, no. 3, p. 15.
7 For another early drawing from before Lamb's arrival in London, see his portrait of Stephen Reynolds apparently drawn in June 1905 (located in the Sidmouth Museum in around 2000; see letter to Henrietta Phipps from Chris Scoble, 12 July 2000 [archive of the artist's family]).
8 In the collection of Felicia Palmer (the artist's daughter) in 1984, see *Henry Lamb* 1984, no. 1, p. 15.
9 *St Euphemia*, c.1454, by Andrea Mantegna, Museo Nazionale di Capodimonte, Naples.
10 Augustus John to Henry Lamb (postmark of 27 July 1907), contained in letters to Henry Lamb, Tate Archive, TAM 15.
11 Konody (see below) is referring here to what he calls 'serious straightforward portraiture', a phase and genre of John's painting that he singles out for particular praise.
12 P.G. Konody, 'New English Art Club', *The Observer,* 18 November 1906. I am extremely grateful to David Boyd-Haycock for providing me with this reference.
13 Henry Lamb to Lytton Strachey, 8 April 1913, Strachey Papers, British Library, vol. XX (ff. i–29).
14 'I saw a young artist called Picasso whose work is wonderful in Paris': Augustus John to Henry Lamb (postmark of 5 June 1907), contained in letters to Henry Lamb, Tate Archive, TAM 15.
15 Augustus John to Henry Lamb (postmark of 17 January 1908), contained in letters to Henry Lamb, Tate Archive, TAM 15.
16 Several envelopes with letters from Augustus John to Henry Lamb (August–September 1907) are addressed 'Mr Henry Lamb/Chez Péron/ Commerçant,/ Doelan': see letters to Henry Lamb, Tate Archive, TAM 15.
17 Frank Rutter, *Sunday Times*, 18 June 1911, quoted by Wendy Baron, *The Camden Town Group*, London, 1979, p. 254.
18 Quoted in Clements 1985, p. 87.
19 Henry Lamb to James Bolivar Manson, 12 November 1912, Tate Archive, TGA 806/1/489-491.
20 *The Daily Telegraph,* 14 December 1911, quoted in Baron 1979, p. 253.
21 *Evening Standard and St James's Gazette,* 6 December 1911, quoted in Baron 1979, p. 254.
22 *The Glasgow Herald*, 4 December 1911, quoted in Baron 1979, p. 254.
23 *Bazaar*, 15 December 1911, quoted in Baron 1979, p. 254.
24 For a particularly detailed critique on the flaws of this painting, see Meuli 1980.
25 Desmond McCarthy, *Eye Witness*, 6 July 1911, quoted in Baron 1979, p. 252.
26 Lamb would characteristically use musical terms when referring to his paintings, particularly in his letters to Strachey: 'The Gola Sonata off my hands, I quickly turned round the sinfonia Gillestica': Henry Lamb to Lytton Strachey, 5 April 1913, Strachey Papers, British Library, vol. XX (ff. i–29).
27 Telephone conversation between the author and Felicia Palmer, 21 December, 2017
28 Stanley Spencer to Henry Lamb, 4 April 1914, Tate Archive, TGA 945.
29 In the collection of J. J. Behrend in 1924; see G. Kennedy, *Henry Lamb*, London, 1924, pl. 20.
30 Henry Lamb document file, Imperial War Museum, London, WA 55/33.
31 Lord Clark to Keith Clements, 22 October 1977, quoted Clements 1985, p. 273.
32 Henry Lamb to E.M.O'R. Dickey, 3 December 1941, Imperial War Museum, London, file #WA 55/33, quoted by Brian Foss, 'No Dead Wood': Henry Lamb and the Canadians, *Canadian Military History*, vol.6/issue 2, Article 7 (2012).
33 Quoted Clements 1985, p. 275.
34 Conversations between Henrietta Phipps and the author, 2013–14.
35 Henry Lamb to Evelyn Waugh, 14 May 1949, Evelyn Waugh Papers, vol. XV, British Library, Add MS 81060: 1929-1965.
36 Keith Clements makes this observation (see Clements 1985, p. 278), also noting that 'in the 1930s he had purchased a Moore carving'.
37 The full title of this work was *Tum tiddly um tum pom pom.* It is sadly lost, known only through contemporary photographs of Nevinson in front of the painting. Ethelbert White's role in this collaboration is rarely acknowledged.
38 See *The Last Romantics: Romantic Tradition in British Art – Burne-Jones to Stanley Spencer*, exh. cat., Barbican Art Gallery, London, 1998.
39 William Gaunt writes in his introduction to *A Memorial Exhibition of Paintings, Drawings and Watercolours by Henry Lamb,* exh. cat., Leicester Galleries, 1961: 'To see the paintings and drawings of Henry Lamb ... in such a comprehensive exhibition as this, is to gain an increased respect for the range and variety of his art, in portraiture what Gainsborough would have called "fancy subjects": in paintings of everyday scenes'.

EARLY WORKS

1

Self-portrait when a young man, c.1906

Pencil on paper, 358 × 254 mm
The Ashmolean Museum, Oxford (purchased, Hope Collection Fund, 1956)

The British artist Sir Lawrence Gowing wrote in his preface to a 1962 exhibition of self-portraits: 'the moment when a man comes to paint himself – he may do it only two or three times in a lifetime, perhaps never – has in the nature of things a special significance'.[1] This was rarely truer than in the case of Henry Lamb. To some extent his career as a painter, its peaks and troughs, its moments of confidence and dejection, can be traced through his self-portraits. It is hard to believe that the present work, almost certainly painted in London in his early days at Augustus John and William Orpen's Chelsea Art School,[2] is by the same artist who executed the competent if workman-like self-portrait with a hat from 1904 (collection of the artist's daughter). The latter seems a vestige of late Victorian/Edwardian painting, competent and well executed – perhaps somewhat in the image of the earlier work of Orpen in particular. This portrait drawing on the other hand is brimming with a fresh confidence, full of youthful chutzpah, unmistakably by a painter who had fallen under the spell of John. If John's influence was one from which Lamb soon sought to distance himself, it is in works like this that the older artist's hand shows itself invaluably helping to move Lamb in the artistic direction he would need to go. Like John before him, Lamb had found a freshness, even modernity, in the Baroque and an admiration for the drawings of Rubens, a constant source of inspiration for these early drawings. Possibly John also encouraged Lamb to change his image, transforming the Manchester medical student into a Bohemian artist, growing a beard and wearing gold earrings. A slightly later portrait, signed and dated 1906, shows the beard now trimmed and the hairstyle dandyishly arranged into an Oscar Wilde-style central parting (private collection).

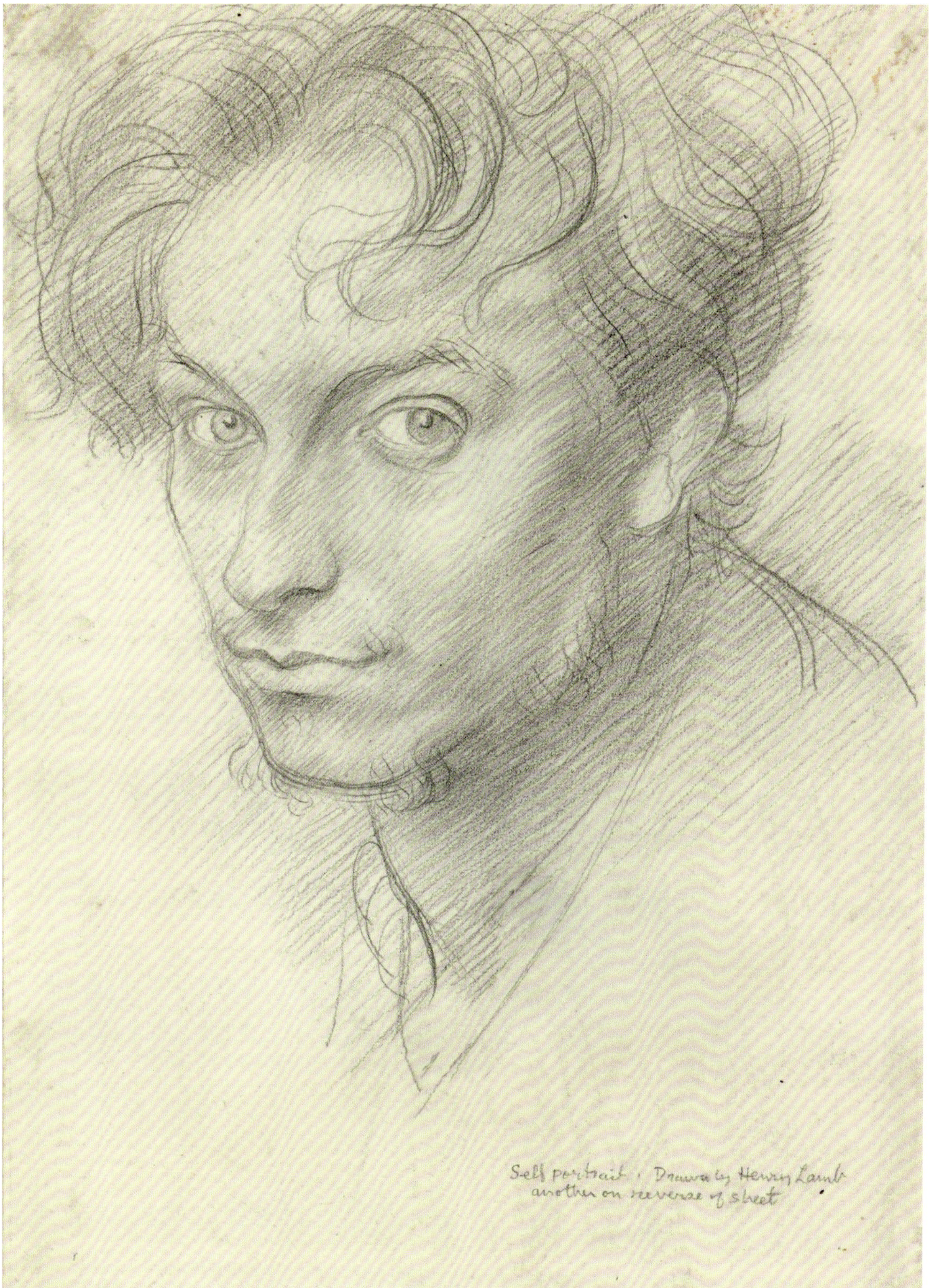
Self portrait. Drawn by Henry Lamb
another on reverse of sheet
Self portrait by Henry Lamb
[over]

2

Euphemia, c.1906

Charcoal on paper, 343 × 263 mm
Private collection

Lamb first met Nina Forrest some time in 1905, taking her to the Manchester University Ball in the summer of that year. In the early 1900s, as throughout his life, the great European Old Masters were never far from his imagination and he re-christened Nina 'Euphemia' since she reminded him of the great painting by Andrea Mantegna of St Euphemia from c.1454 in the Museo Nazionale di Capodimonte in Naples. Lamb married Euphemia in 1906 and, although the pair were legally married until 1928 (when Lamb sought a divorce in order to marry Pansy), the union itself would prove both short-lived and stormy. Euphemia soon became known as one of the most alluring and enigmatic artist's muses of her age, all the more enigmatic perhaps because of her background, which remained shadowy. Euphemia became a significant model for numerous notable artists of the era, among them Augustus John (with whom she was closely involved in the period very soon after the failure of her marriage to Lamb), James Dickson Innes, Jacob Epstein and Ambrose McEvoy. She was also married to Edward Gore for a few years in the mid 1930s. In the present drawing, as in other sketches from the mid 1900s, it is the influence of Augustus John that is most apparent.

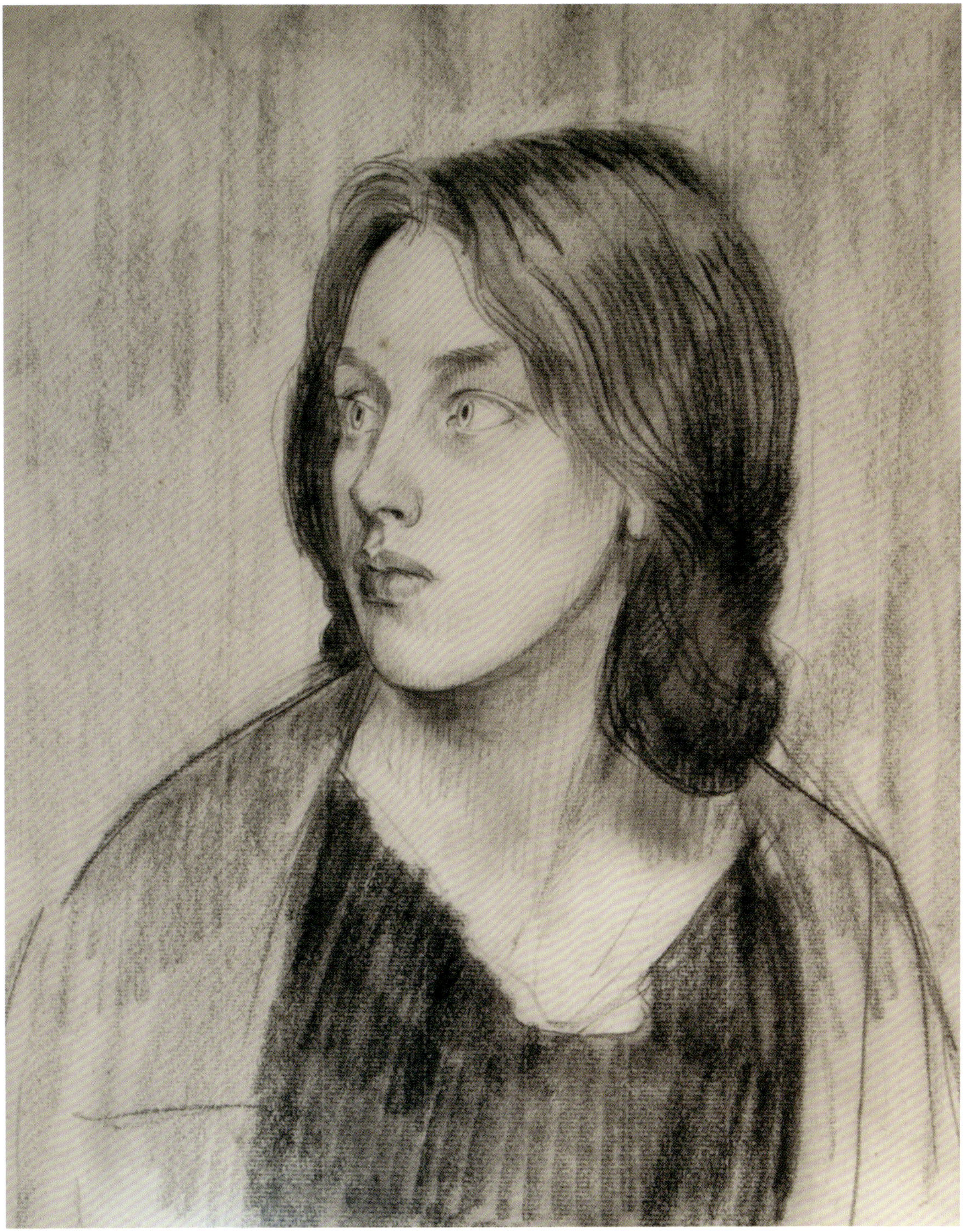

3

Breton Youth, 1910

Oil on panel, 33.5 × 24.1 cm
Bolton Library and Museum Services (acquired with assistance from the Victoria and Albert Museum, 1985)

Some of Lamb's earliest mature and non-'John-influenced' attempts at oil painting date from his time staying with the Favennec family in Doëlan near Pont Aven in 1910. Indeed *Breton Youth* is a work that is immediately reminiscent of Gauguin. Lamb could not have been unaware of the French artist's trips to the area and would have seen his work both while in Paris in 1907 and through exhibitions in London in 1908 and 1909. Keith Clements refers to such works as 'at a glance, so reminiscent of Gauguin ... it seems as if the master himself had been beside Henry'.[3] Another influence may have been Aristide Maillol, who, although better known as a sculptor, executed comparable portrait heads, such as that of his wife in 1894. George Kennedy on the other hand in 1924 explicitly relates *Breton Youth* to Picasso, and, if seen in the context of *Phantasy* (cat. 10) in the following year, this could be accepted as an equally compelling comparison.[4] Villagers at Doëlan did not recognize the sitter of *Breton Youth,* and Clements has commented that the work was 'less a portrait in any conventional sense and more a starting point for stylistic experiment'.[5] Letters to Lytton Strachey, however, suggest that Lamb identified the work as a portrait of one of the Favennec children, probably Ernest (born 1890).[6] The work also appears to have been one of the artist's early exhibits as a member of the Camden Town Group, being shown at the group's exhibition in June 1911 (probably as no. 22).

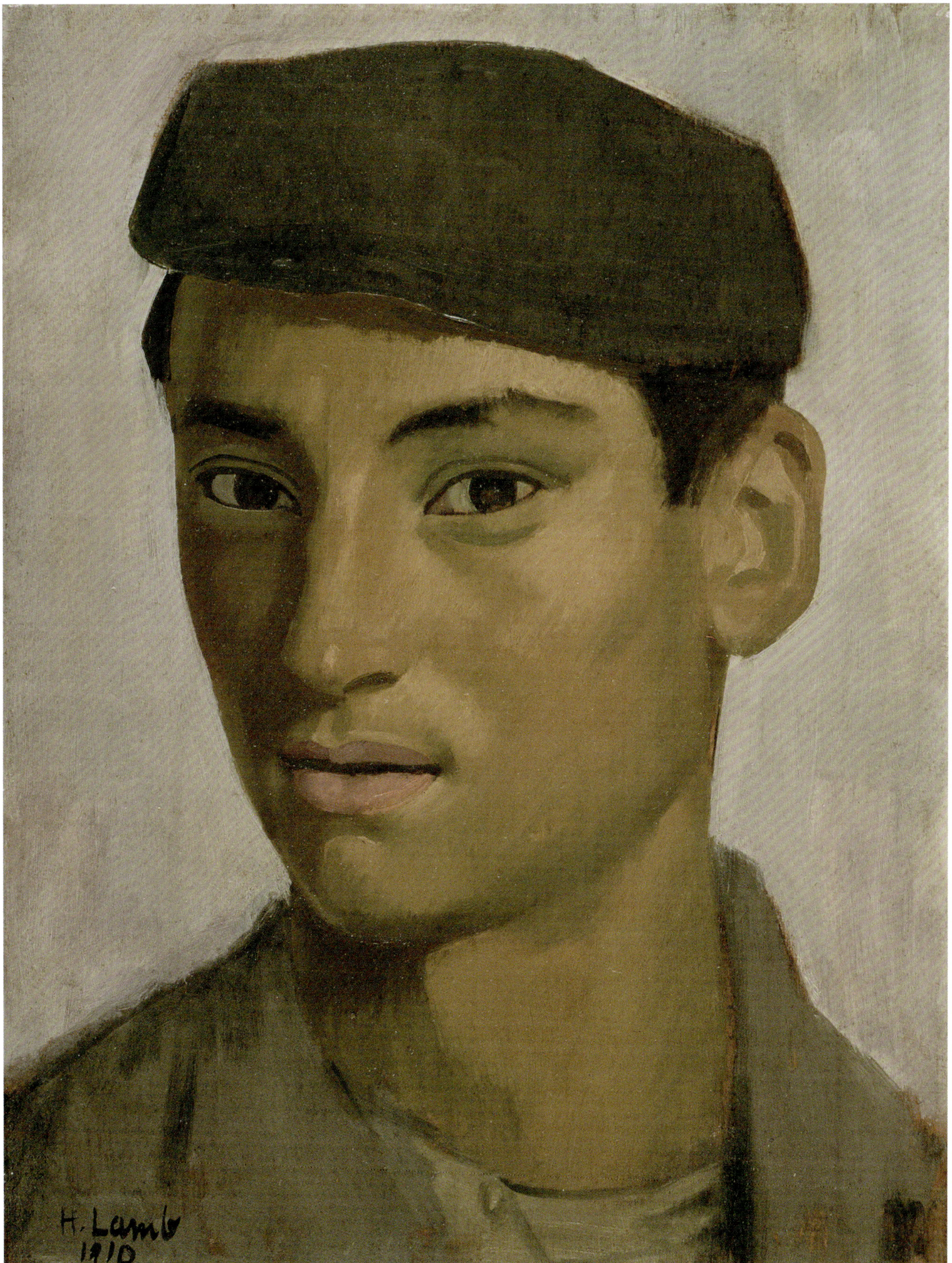
H. Lamb
1910

4
Death of a Peasant, 1911

Oil on canvas, 36.8 × 31.8 cm
Tate (Presented by the Trustees of the Chantrey Bequest, 1944, N05630)

The death of Madame Favennec occurred during the artist's first and most artistically significant stay at Kersimon in Doëlan during the summer of 1910. A mother of twelve and matriarch of a family that Lamb would take to his heart, she had endured the agony of throat cancer and the emaciation of a body that could no longer take food. The event had a profound effect on Lamb, who painted this scene on his return to England in the middle of 1911. He subsequently showed it at 19 Fitzroy Street, where, promoted by Sickert, it was probably acquired by Sir Michael Sadler. Lamb painted a second version soon afterwards in tempera, which, as the artist's favourite, was more widely exhibited.

Contemporary criticism confirms *Death of a Peasant* as Lamb's first major success, Frank Rutter subsequently referring to it as 'His modern pietà ... the first great tragic picture England produced in the twentieth century'.[7] The picture's direct and uncompromising impact is in no small part due to the intense focus on its central subjects at the expense of background and other incidental detail. The depiction of both dying mother, foreshortened so as to raise her face to the level of the viewer, and the grief-stricken husband are depicted with an expressionist intensity, which, unlike some of Lamb's work, never verges on the caricature. Though superficially Gauguinesque in its execution, it is the European Old Master tradition that is most often cited as the prime inspiration for this, one of the artist's more modern images. A startling comparison has been made to a work of one of his great heroes, Andrea Mantegna, and his *Dead Christ and Three Mourners* of c.1480 in the Pinacoteca di Brera in Milan.[8] Keith Clements has also talked of the impact of the Northern Renaissance and the emotional intensity seen in works by artists such as Matthias Grünewald and Flemish painters of the sixteenth century. Some vestige of knowledge from his Manchester medical training may also account for his candid observation of the woman's condition. Such persuasive arguments suggest that there is more nuance in the influences on Henry Lamb, the emerging painter, than the more geographically obvious one of Paul Gauguin.

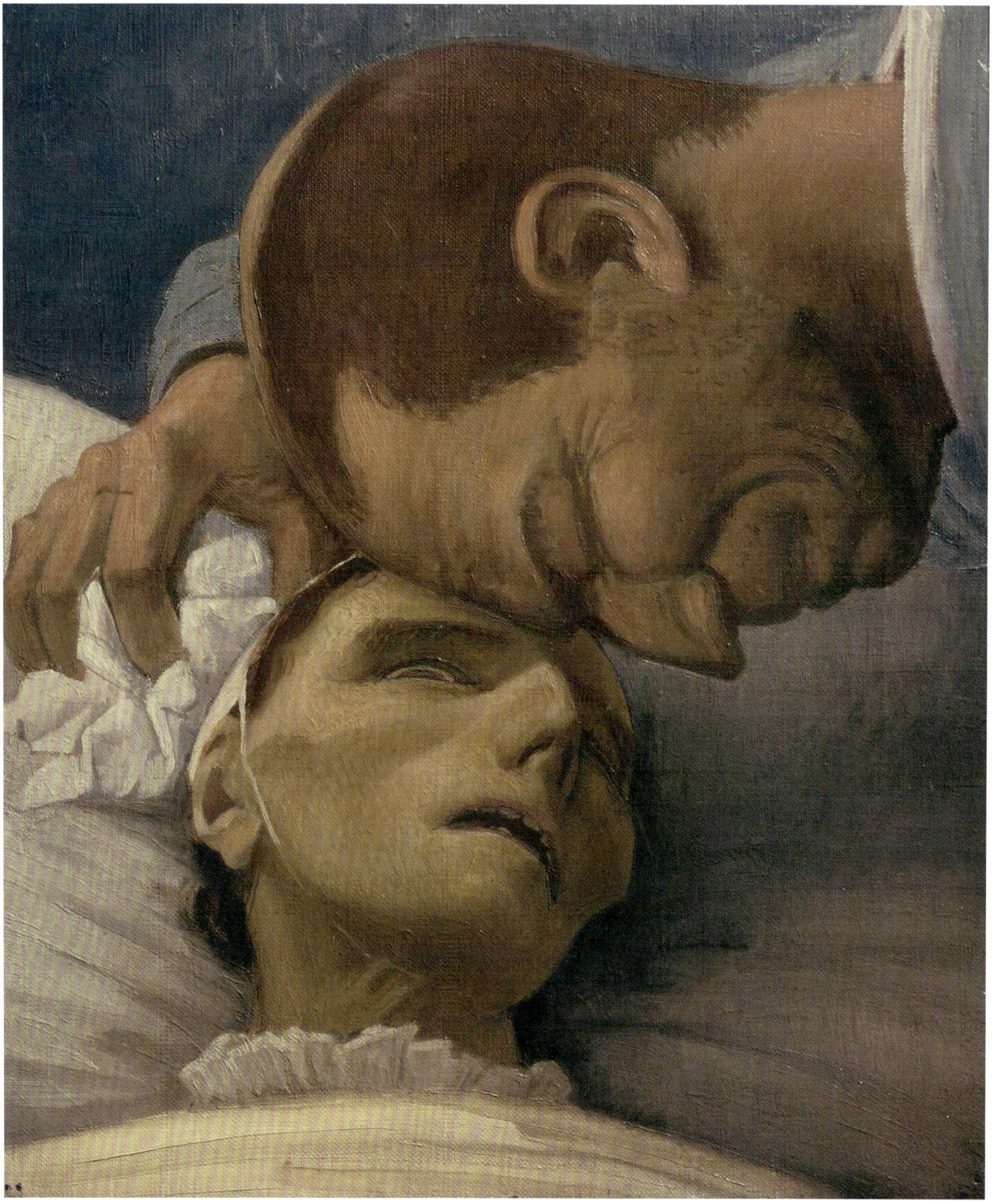

5

Study for *A Breton Pardon*, c.1911

Blue-grey wash over pen and ink on paper, 335 × 277 mm
The Henry Lamb Estate

The entry on the finished painting that derives from this study in the Manchester City Art Gallery catalogue claims *Breton Pardon* as 'the most complex and Gauguinesque of Lamb's Breton compositions'.[9] Certainly the primitive stylization in the rendering of the worshippers' faces is strongly reminiscent of Gauguin but, as so often with Lamb, the overall result is a perplexing cocktail of diverse influences. This more subdued and careful outline study is revealing in suggesting a more traditional source for the work in the French Realist tradition of the later nineteenth century – the work of Jules Breton and Pascal Dagnan-Bouveret, for example. Lamb may also have had some knowledge of other British painters who had travelled to Brittany, amongst them the Cornish artist Norman Garstin, of whom he would have been aware at the New English Art Club and whose *Breton Parade* (painted perhaps later in 1913) has some affinity with this work. The painting depicts the quintessentially Breton ceremony of the Pardon. Typically a form of pilgrimage, the Pardon is a penitential ceremony central to Breton Catholicism, usually occurring on the feast day of the saint of a church. The day begins with a Mass at 4 am, with the confession and rosary being recited on their way to the place of pilgrimage. Lamb's work depicts the crowd as it enters the church almost as a single abstract form, effectively conveying the sense of communal rituality that is central to the event. Following the church service there is a grand procession which takes place around the church.

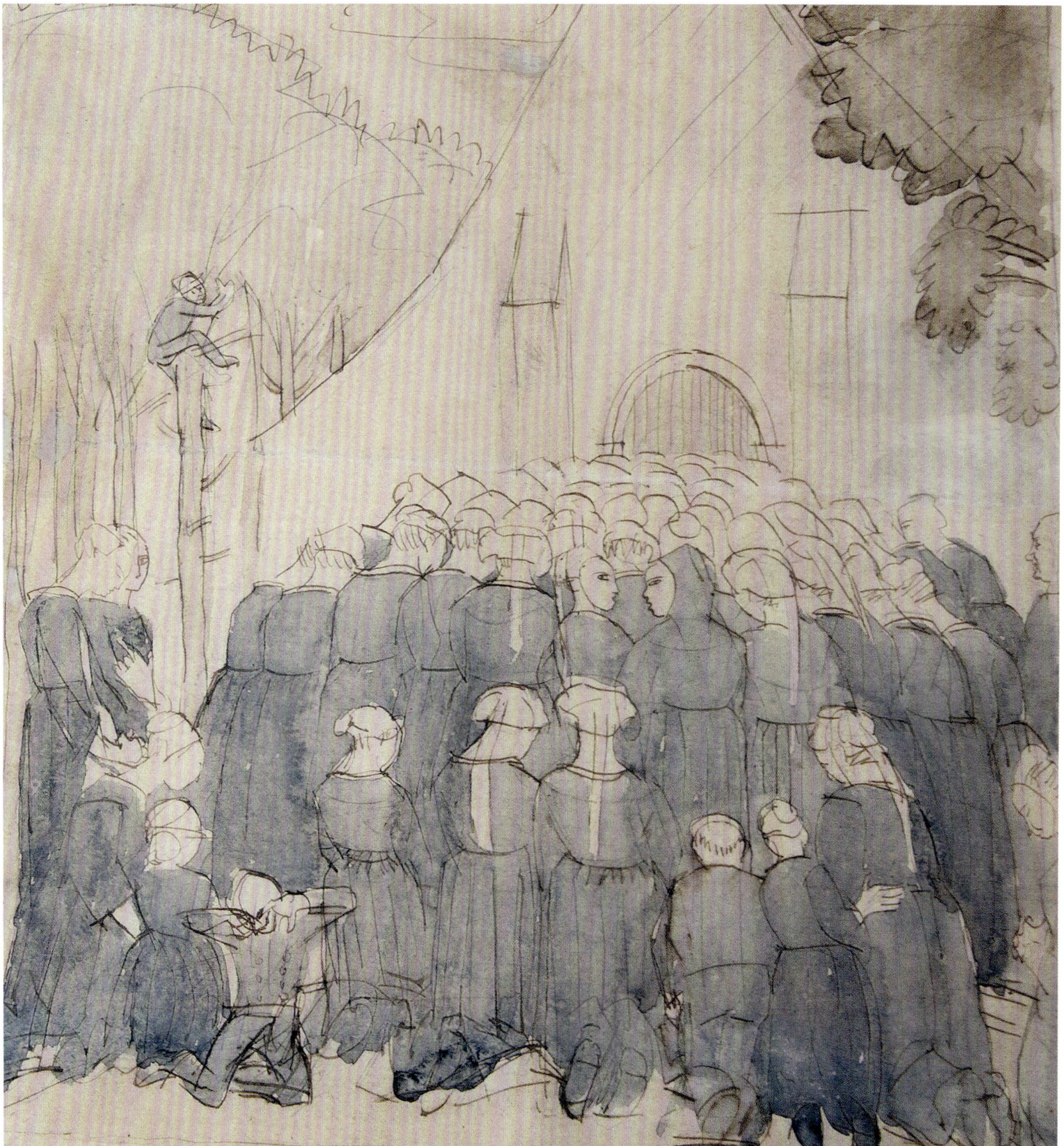

6

The Lady with Lizards, c.1911

Oil on canvas, 51.5 × 40.9 cm
Manchester City Art Gallery (Gift from the Contemporary Art Society, 1954)

Perhaps owing to her presence in Brittany at around the same date, the present painting has been mistakenly identified as a portrait of Edie McNeill. A drawing of this sitter labelled by the artist *Baker's Wife*, however, together with a pendant painting *Girl of the Fields* (formerly in the collection of Sir David Scott)[10] suggests otherwise, and both works point to the constant experimentation in Lamb's style in the years before the First World War. As with *Girl of the Fields*, Lamb places his sitter against a highly decorative tapestry-like landscape, which appears flattened and stylized. In such works he is perhaps superficially at his closest to the more decorative style of Bloomsbury painters, with whom he would soon have a brief artistic dalliance through his inclusion in the second Post-Impressionist exhibition of 1912. Despite this, the modelling of the sitter in *The Lady with Lizards* is altogether more traditional, fashioning a style less like Gauguin and more like his own form of English classicism that would characterize the later Breton pieces and the great Irish paintings of the following year.

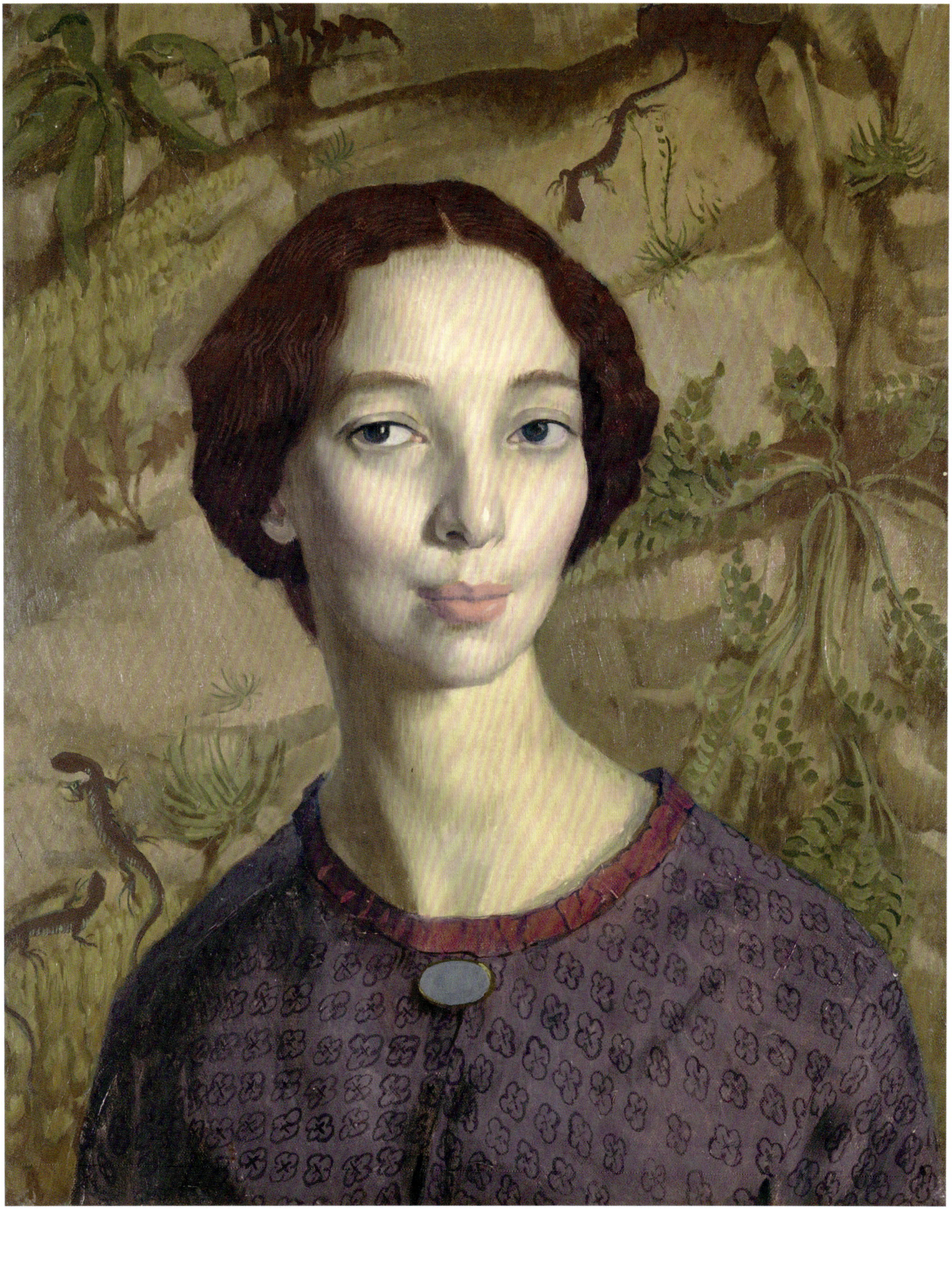

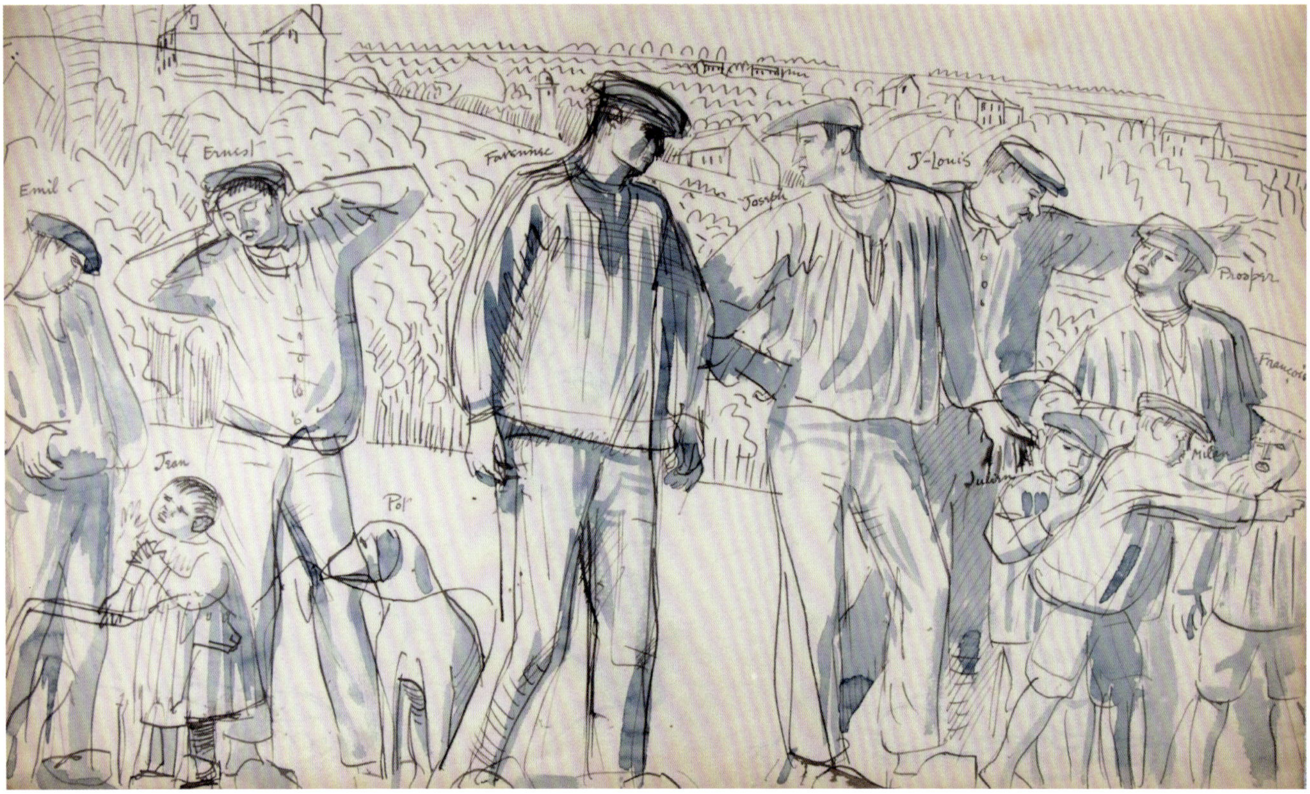

7

Study for a Favennec family portrait group, c.1911

From a sketchbook of the artist of c.1911
Pen and ink on paper (across two sheets), 330 × 270 mm each
The Henry Lamb Estate

This carefully labelled compositional study from one of the artist's larger Breton sketchbooks hints at the more ambitious compositions he may have had in mind during his time in France. With a few notable exceptions, such as *A Breton Pardon* from around the same date, Lamb would rarely attempt a sophisticated conversation piece until *Fisherfolk, Gola Island* in 1913 (cat. 11). It is not surprising, however, that ideas for them formed themselves in the many pages of the sketchbooks he used during his time abroad. The present sheet is an idea for a group of the male members of the Favennec family set against a panorama of the Breton countryside. It is unclear whether this is a whimsical study or the germ of an idea for a larger picture. Lamb remained devoted to many members of the family, but he enjoyed the most intellectual relationship with Jean-Louis (middle left), with whom he would discuss history, art and politics. In letters to Lytton Strachey Lamb shared in the pure beauty he saw in some of the younger boys – '... as for Prosper he has become 190 times more beautiful',[11] and of his portrait of Ernest Favennec he wrote: '... wouldn't you like to have jumped behind him'.[12]

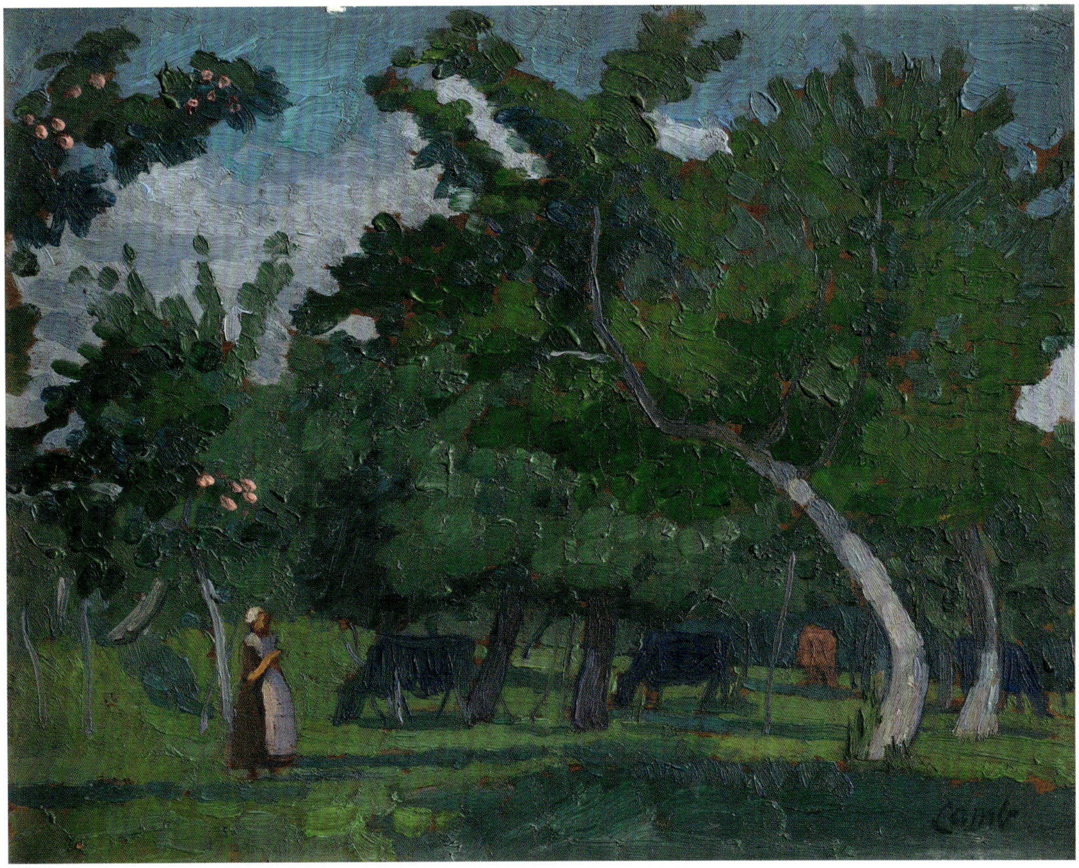

8

Orchard in Brittany, c.1911

Oil on panel, 18 × 23.5 cm
Homerton College, University of Cambridge

Few works exist in Lamb's output from his Brittany period that can be termed pure landscape. On his visit to Donegal in 1912, however, landscape *pochades*, small on-the-spot oil sketches, of the Irish coast were a more significant part of his output and suggest a natural ability at working *en plein air* that is rarely evident in his post-war work. *Orchard in Brittany* is firmly in the spirit of Augustus John's domestic landscapes from around the same period, and, in his letters to Strachey, Lamb recalls visiting the John family in their new home, Alderney Manor, in 1911: 'Fairly consoled by having a surprise time with Dorelia. She lives in an amazing place ... a vast secluded park of prairies ... pine woods and birchwoods ... lovely naked boys running about the woods'.[13] John's panel landscape sketches from the period are rarely without figures, his free-living family frequently seen out in the open air and at play. The present work also belongs in this genre – Lamb's new Doëlan 'family' in evidence in the form of one of the Favennec's older daughters, possibly Marie-Joseph, in amongst the family's herd of cattle.

9
Edie McNeill, 1911

Oil on canvas, 127.5 × 76.2 cm
Southampton City Art Gallery

Dorelia's sister Edie McNeill had been the sitter in two of Lamb's most successful early portraits, *Portrait of Edie McNeill: Purple and Gold* from c.1910 and his recently re-discovered *Portrait of Edie McNeill in a Hat* from 1909 (formerly in the collection of Cpt. John Crawford Flitch).[14] It is perhaps unsurprising that in an attempt to re-visit this success he decided to bring Edie out with him to stay with the Favennecs in Doëlan in July 1911. This outcome was to prove a far cry from the triumph he expected. He wrote to Strachey on 24 July 1911: 'A sudden enterprise made me carry off Dorelia's sister with me. I thought the main thing was to have a sitter always handy and how I have groaned since'.[15] In contrast to Dorelia, whose company he found constantly engaging and stimulating, Edie he felt to be dull and inefficient and her manner slovenly. The present portrait is the primary result of this time together, a picture that has sometimes been regarded as both awkward and unsatisfactorily resolved – not unlike their relationship. By mid August Lamb had already acknowledged that his own indecision on the picture and its composition had led to a dissatisfying conclusion: 'My *ménage* ... cannot be broken up until a large portrait of this woman is finished ... [it] began [so] sublimely that I was of course too intimidated not to spoil it afterwards but most of the sublimity was accidental'.[16]

The main criticism of the work has been levelled against the background, the *Times* critic on its first showing at the New English Art Club in the autumn of that year observing: '... he has failed to find a convention for the sky, and it looks both empty and literal'.[17] Evidence from the artist's sketchbooks suggest he had at one time conceived the portrait against a rolling Breton landscape, also experimenting with the direction of Edie's figure, the aloof averted gaze of the final painting perhaps indicative of the couple's fractious relationship. Even if the 1911 portrait fails where the slickly executed early depictions of this sitter succeed, it could be said to have a more important place in the development of Lamb's style. The shadows of Orpen and John loom large in the two earlier portraits, and although the present work has been likened (particularly in the preparatory sketches) to John's depictions of Dorelia standing this comparison falls short in respect of the picture's execution. Although some of the contemporary criticism of the work identified its shortcomings, elsewhere the painting was celebrated as a resounding success, and it is not unreasonable to suspect that this helped to encourage a renewed confidence in the young artist.[18] Here Lamb was introducing a more tightly painted, subtly stylized technique, working towards a blend of figure and landscape, which, without works like this portrait, would never have led to the satisfying synthesis seen in his masterpiece, *Fisherfolk, Gola Island*, two years later (cat. 11).

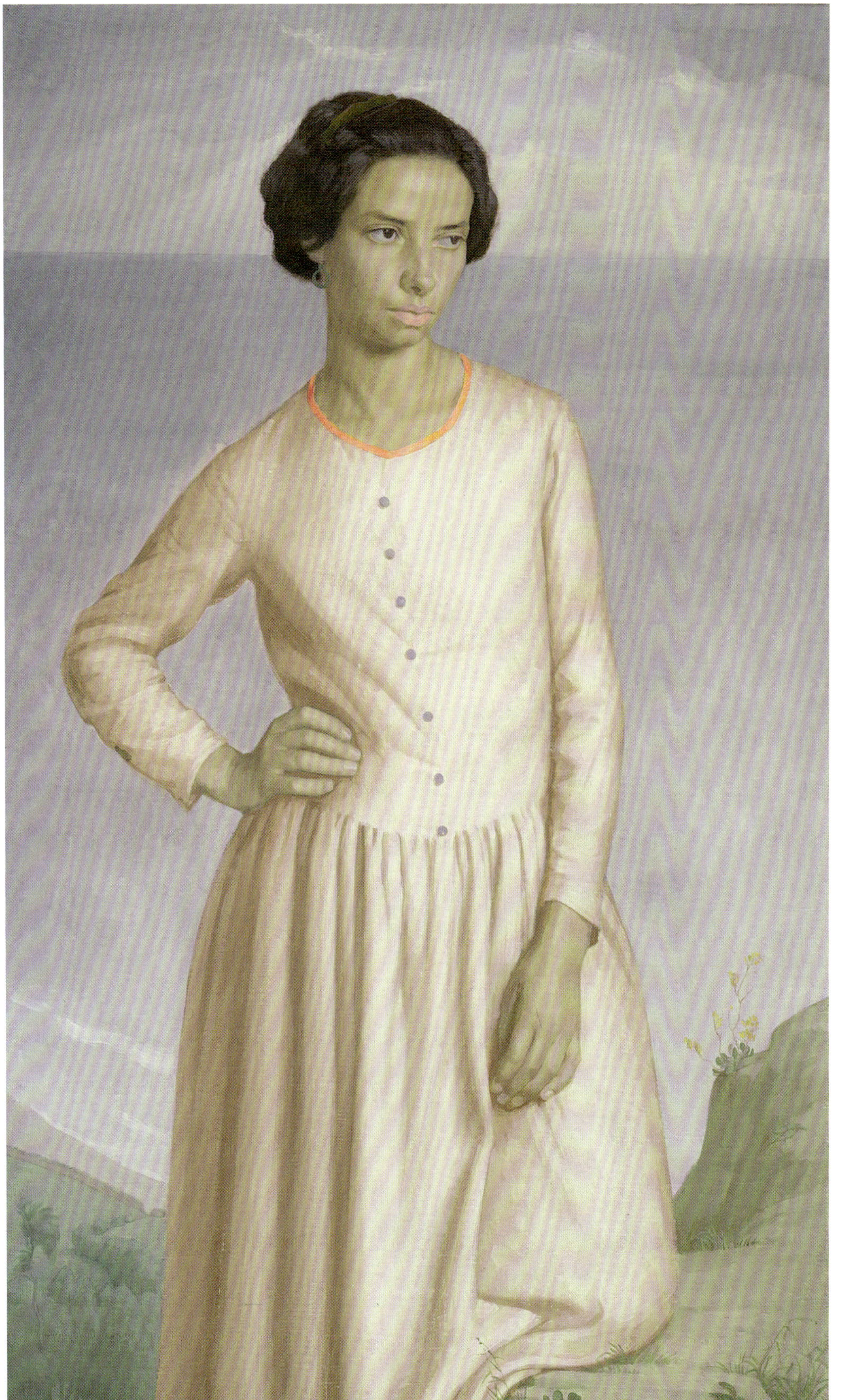

10

Phantasy, 1912

Oil on canvas, 86.5 × 61 cm
Tate (Presented by the Contemporary Arts Society, 1924, N03840)

Lamb was a huge admirer of the early work of Picasso (he made no secret, on the other hand, of his dislike for Picasso's great contemporary Matisse). Even if he never met the Spanish artist he had numerous opportunities to view his work – at exhibitions in Paris in 1907 and 1908, for example, and on visits to Parisian art dealers. In 1912 he would see his work at the Second Post-Impressionist Exhibition in London. The phase of Picasso's work that would attract Lamb particularly was the style that emerged from the Blue and Rose periods, and in particular the horse and rider theme. Nowhere is this more apparent than in *Phantasy*. The idea for the subject appears to have emerged from a series of earlier life studies of the male nude (mainly in chalks and on blue paper), some of which are in the collection of the artist's family. Lamb regularly wrote of his frustration with life drawing and of accurately depicting the male nude in particular, but the end result in this painting is surprisingly successful. Lamb would take these themes and styles no further, perhaps in part owing to reviews that suggested too overt an influence from Picasso's stable. On its first showing at the New English Art Club in the summer of 1912 *The Times* reviewer referred to it as 'very clever .... These two nude figures with a horse come from M. Picasso .... But Mr Lamb seems to have taken the theme without knowing clearly what it meant, and the picture is an expression of his taste in art rather than his feeling towards nature.'[19] In a more prosaic footnote to the work's equestrian inspiration, the artist later commented that *Phantasy* was painted 'when I was riding a good deal'.[20]

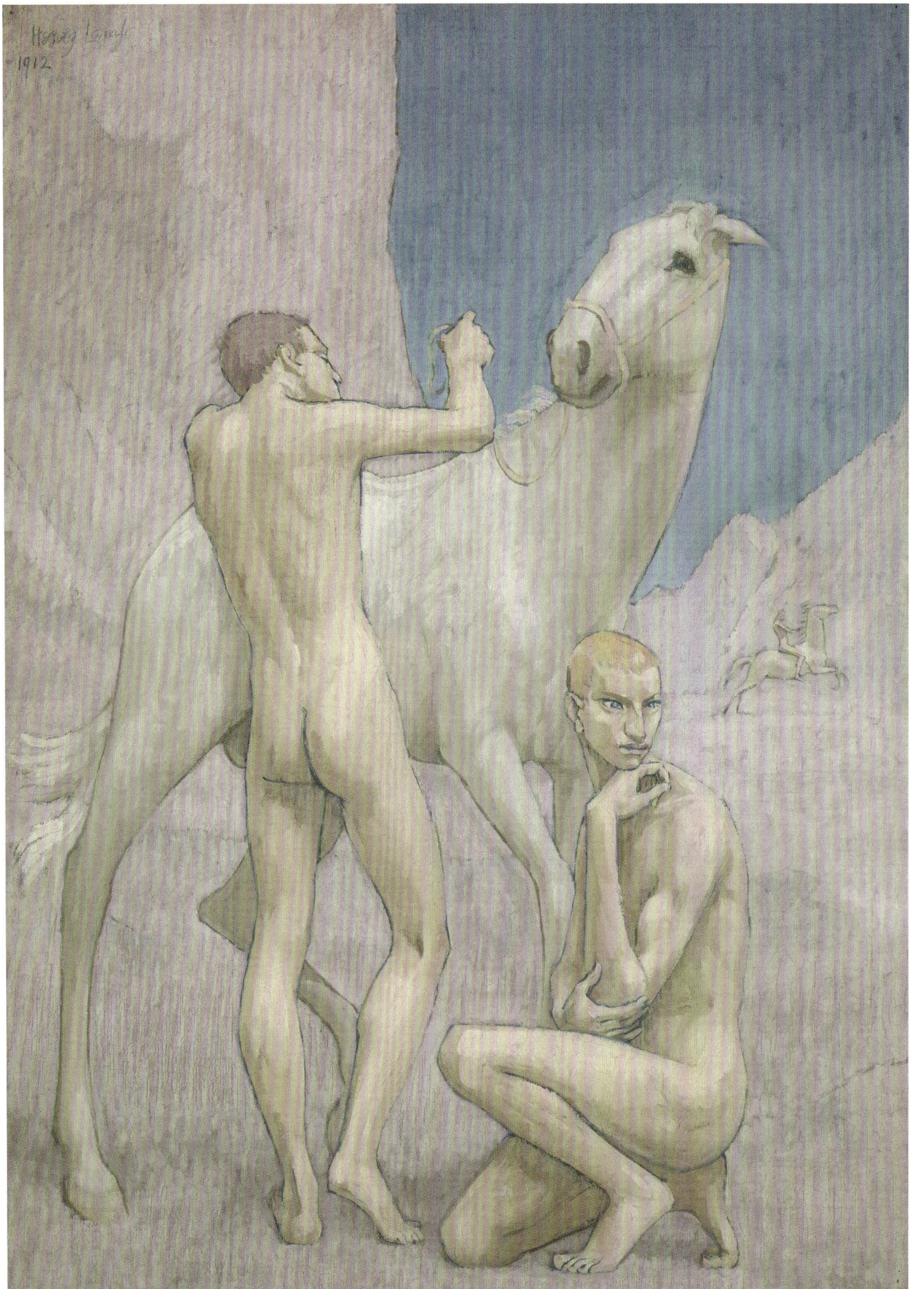
1912

11

Fisherfolk, Gola Island, 1913

Oil on canvas, 82.1 × 102.6 cm
Private collection

At the suggestion of his friend George Kennedy and in a self-conscious attempt to replicate his experiences at Doëlan, Lamb made his first trip to the Donegal coast in August 1912. As with so many of his ventures, it was an experience that would provide him with ups and downs, fallow stretches of painter's block and seesaws of emotion. Initially staying in Middletown off the middle-northwest edge of Donegal's rugged coast, Lamb struggled to find patient sitters, needing to use his camera instead to provide subject matter. It was here that he learned of Gola Island. Remote and primitive and lying a mile off the Donegal coast, the island had a fast falling population of only 169 people in 1911 (a year before Lamb's trip). The island made an immediate impact on the artist, and he wrote to Strachey: 'Gola has become a promised land for me – surely I never saw such beauties as before – easily eclipsing the Bretons: & then the colours !'[21] Finding lodgings with the McGinley family, he spent much of October there, although the wild winds prevented him from sketching outdoors. As with many other trips of this type, Lamb's correspondence from Gola both in 1912 and on his return to the island in August 1913 was largely a catalogue of complaints, principally centred on the weather, poor light and his own ill health. It was such factors that led him famously to refer to it, in a letter to Lady Ottoline Morrell, as his 'half dreaded exile'. His reaction to the island swayed from day to day: on 22 August he referred to 'the terrifying gloom of this place',[22] while a week later 'the ancient nursery charms of the island society have again made their calm way into my hurried soul … it is in fact an Elysian spot'.[23] Further letters suggest a slow progress, punctuated by occasional landscape sketches and head studies. It appears that it was the pressure of leaving and the end of the harvest that finally pushed Lamb into action, writing to Strachey on 11 October: 'the potato crop is just coming to an end & at last the sitters are available: I could get all the studies I want for a picture'.[24]

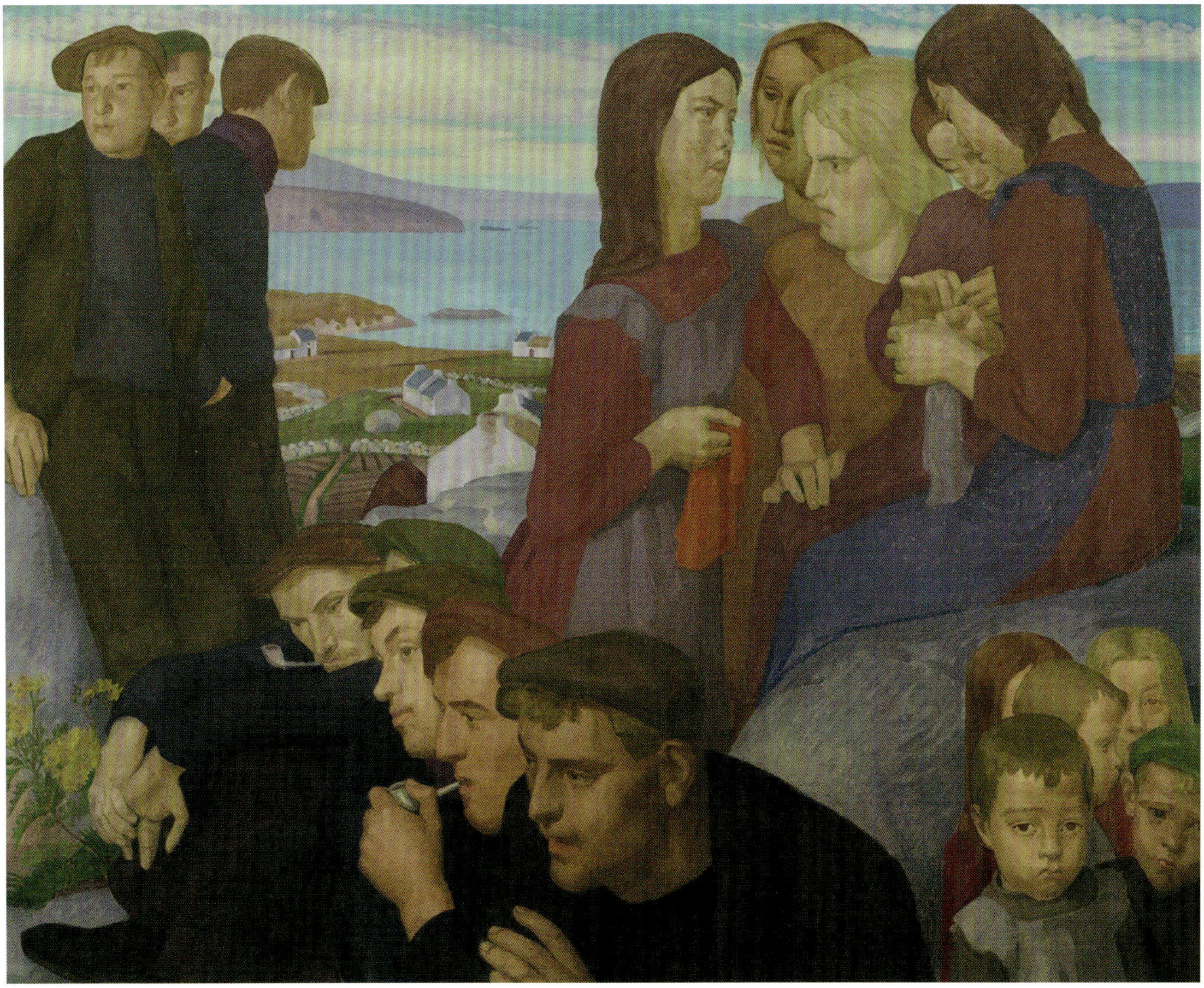

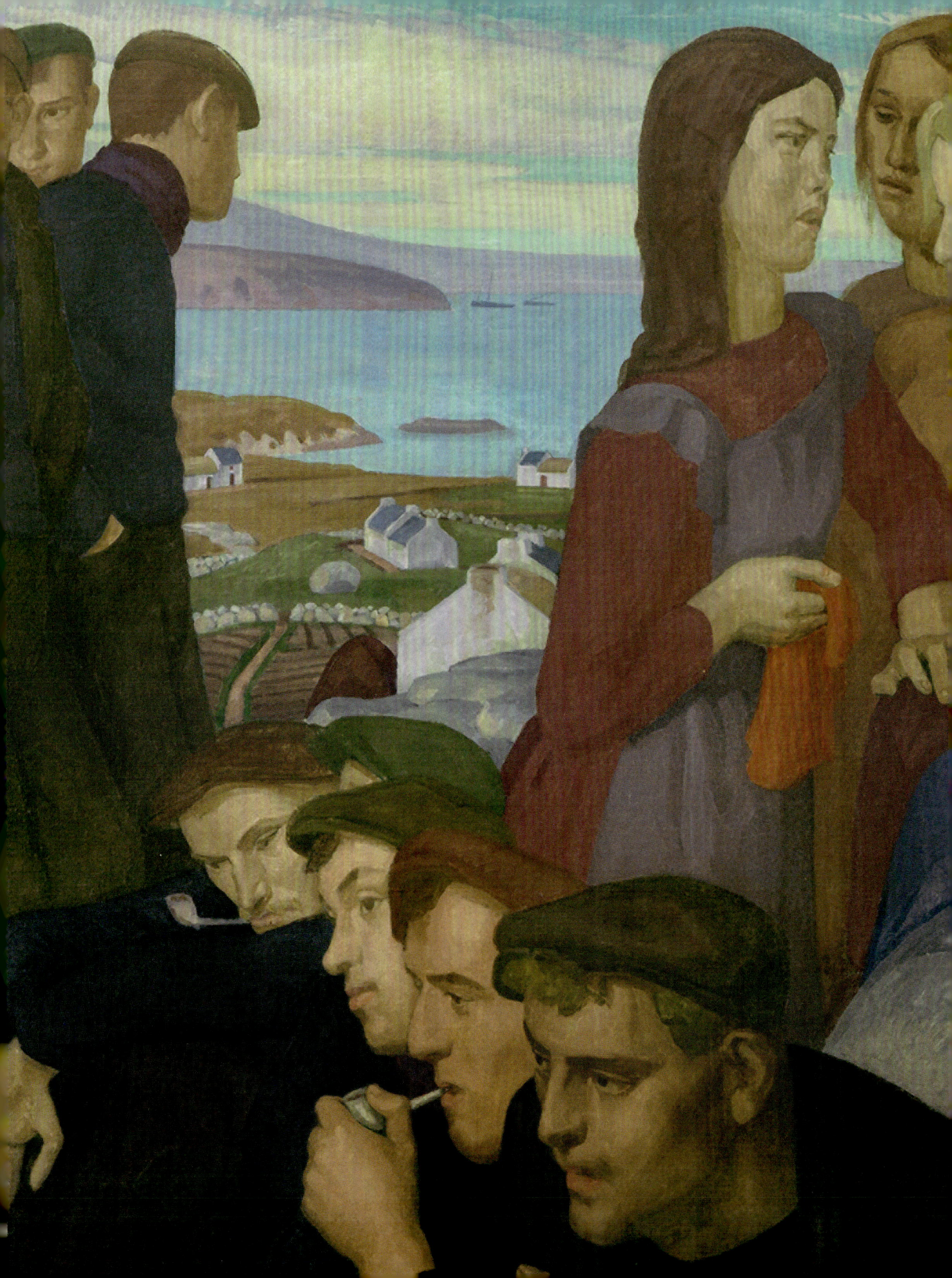

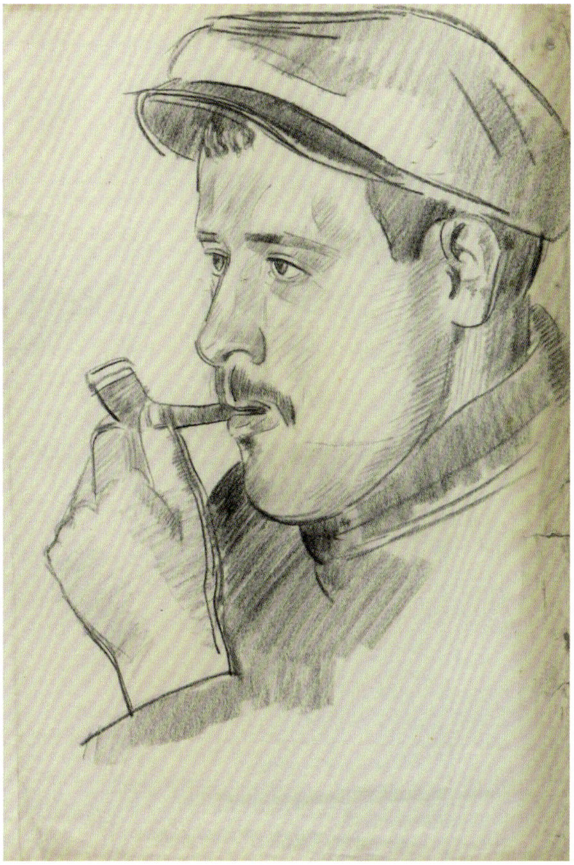

FIG. 12
Study for *Fisherfolk, Gola Island*
Pencil on paper, 360 × 235 mm
The Henry Lamb Estate

Lamb seems to have made several significant compositions from his time in Gola, exhibiting *Group among Rocks, Donegal* at the Twentieth Century Art Exhibition at the Whitechapel Art Gallery in 1914 (no. 363) and another called *Island Parliament,* untraced but possibly related to the present work. He also made some gritty depictions of islanders working on the potato crop and re-worked the present idea for the near identical *Souvenir of Donegal* in 1953.[25] It is *Fisherfolk, Gola Island,* though, that would prove the fulfillment of his Irish experiences. One of the artist's true masterpieces, it would emerge from a mist of agonizingly slow progress and false starts (as with his other great successes). A serenely poetic work, transforming the earthy Donegal landscape into an other-worldly paradise, *Fisherfolk* is also most distinctively 'Lamb' in style: even if there are traceable passages of significant influences – from the French Symbolist Maurice Denis, for example – its warmly muted palette and bleak Irish setting place it firmly in quite another world. Through its sophisticated composition of figures, seemingly at one with their landscape, emerges the art form that would prove the artist's most successful in the following decade – the group portrait.

12

Self-portrait, 1914

Oil on panel, 36.8 × 31.8 cm
National Portrait Gallery, London (Given by Darsie Japp)

The *Self-portrait* of 1914 is the artist's most startling and supremely confident work in the genre. After he had wrested himself away from the influence of Augustus John (so apparent in the self-portrait drawings of 1905 and 1906), it is indicative of a new-found freedom and confidence that would occasionally reveal itself in the post-war years. Painted just before he was enlisted as a dresser for outpatients at Guy's Hospital (for which he was required to cut his hair short), it was executed in the wake of his finest works, which included *Fisherfolk, Gola Island* from the previous year (cat. 11) and the portrait *Lytton Strachey* (fig. 1), which lay unfinished in his studio at the Vale of Health in Hampstead awaiting its final completion at the end of the War. As a work it also shows the mark of his meeting with Stanley Spencer late in the previous year. Spencer's own startling *Self-portrait* of 1914 (Tate) shares some notable parallels with the present work. Similarly uncompromising and a statement of his arrival as an artist, Spencer appears to look at the viewer with an even more direct gaze. In both portraits the right side of the face is theatrically obscured by shadow. 1914 would prove a careering-changing year for Lamb and Spencer, as it would for many artists from their feted generation. Soon both men would take up medical posts in a war that was deeply to affect them but also present them with opportunities that would partly define them as artists in the inter-war years.

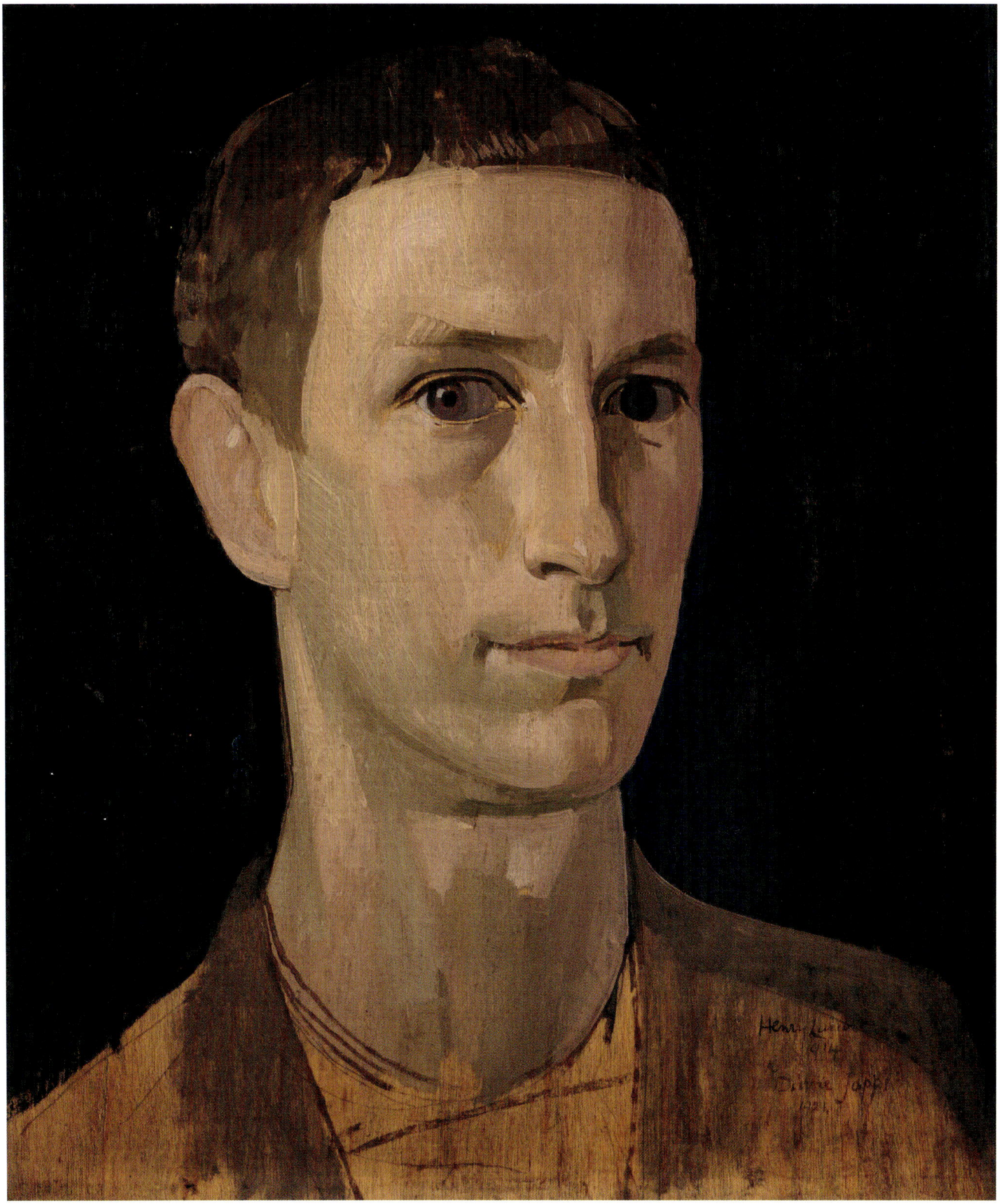

13

Landscape in the Judaean Hills, c.1917

Pencil on paper, 205 × 330 mm
The Henry Lamb Estate

Apart from a couple of small sketchbooks in the possession of the artist's family, showing medical staff and recuperating soldiers at Fécamp, and an isolated watercolour of soldiers playing a card game, *Cards before 'Stand-to', Palestine* (formerly in the collection of the artist's family), Lamb's First World War work is unusual in its conspicuous lack of human elements. Here, despite their artistic and personal closeness at this date, he differs from Spencer, who illustrates letters with quirky elements of working army life and writes of sketching heads of soldiers. Lamb's medical duties appear to have allowed him next to no time to devote to art, and little of significance came out of his time as a serving soldier. Once in Palestine, whither he was transferred from Macedonia in 1917, his surviving work hints at an interest in the open vistas and rocky landscapes of the country, or the minutiae of the fauna. Such detailed landscape sketches as the present work are generally pages taken from a small number of surviving sketchbooks. Almost Pre-Raphaelite in intensity, recalling the Palestinian landscapes of William Holman Hunt, they retain a miniature power that is generally lacking in his larger painted landscapes.

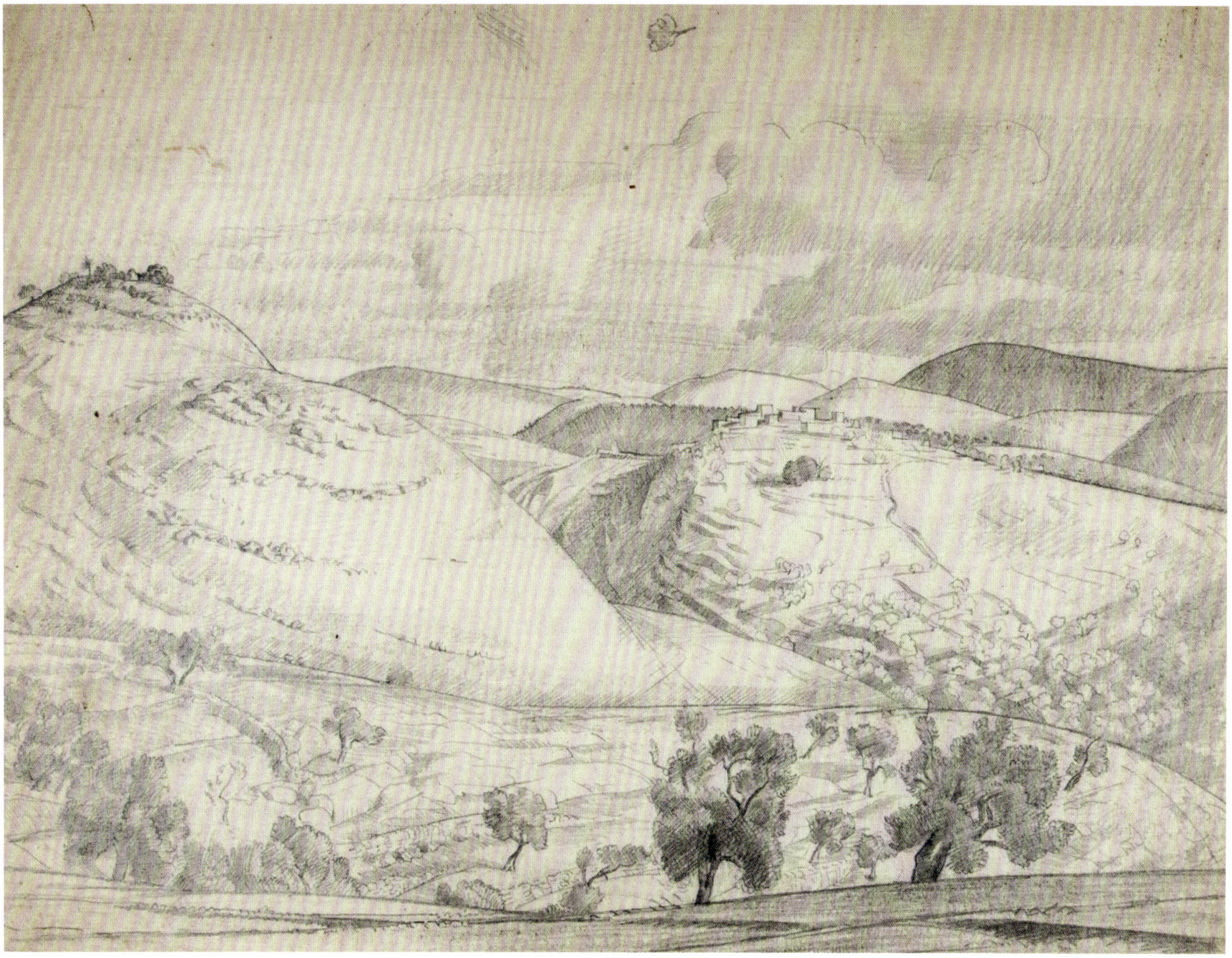

14

Irish Troops in the Judaean Hills Surprised by a Turkish Bombardment, 1919

Oil on canvas, 183.4 × 219.7 cm
Imperial War Museums
SALISBURY ONLY

Lamb was serving as a medical officer with the 5th Inniskilling Fusiliers in May 1918 when the events that are represented in this painting took place. Turkish artillery had ambushed British positions near the village of Jililya in Palestine. The regiment lost five men in the assault, and Lamb, commended for his 'magnificent bravery' caring for the wounded, was subsequently awarded the Military Cross.

Like many of the greatest paintings that were completed following the First World War, *Irish Troops* was in fact executed some time after the events depicted. It was a commission for the ultimately unrealised Hall of Remembrance that had been proposed following the Armistice in 1918. To help ensure the visual unity of the scheme, artists were actively encouraged to work in pairs in an open sharing of ideas. It is for this reason that notable similarities emerge between *Irish Troops* and Stanley Spencer's contribution to the scheme, *Travoys Arriving with Wounded at a Dressing-Station at Smol, Macedonia, September 1916*, particularly in respect of the steep overhead vantage points and high horizons in both works. The extent to which one influenced the other has been the subject of continual debate. Spencer and Lamb enjoyed a long correspondence throughout the War and even found themselves in close proximity during active service in Macedonia and Salonika. Frustratingly, though, little of this correspondence dates from the period immediately after the War, when the artists were working on their respective war paintings.

Despite this, even a brief reading of their earlier letters could not fail to note the significant part that European painting of the fifteenth and sixteenth century played in their exchanges. Such influences are constantly apparent in Spencer's work of the date, and are no less evident in *Irish Troops*. A particular comparison can be made between Lamb's awkward and dramatically foreshortened figures – recoiling from the blast, heaving away the wounded or lying lifeless on the ground – and Paolo Uccello's depictions of soldiers in his three panels of *The Battle of San Romano*. This was the work that had inspired the Hall of Remembrance scheme in the first place, and Lamb would have known at least two of the series – in the National Gallery in London and in the Louvre in Paris. Like Uccello's *Battle*, Lamb's painting is a work of drama, a chilling snapshot of a particular event, an isolated moment of violence in a war that had so many. This characteristic was picked up by the *Times* writer, in one of many positive reviews of the work following its appearance alongside other war pictures from the scheme at the Royal Academy in December 1919, describing its subject as 'so treated as to suggest a momentary arrest of time in which apparently irrelevant details are stamped upon the mind'. As a work of reportage it is distinct from any other wartime work

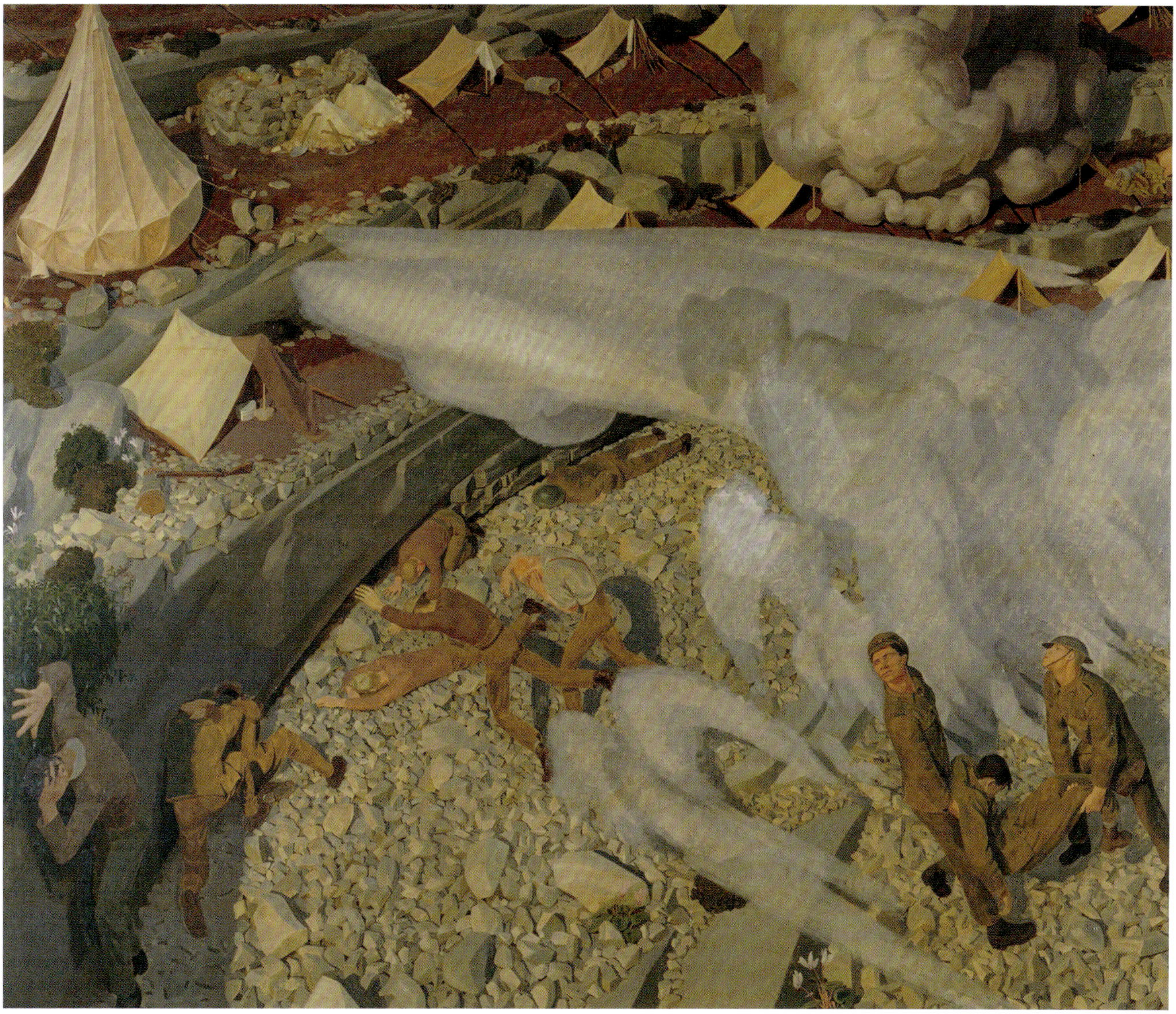

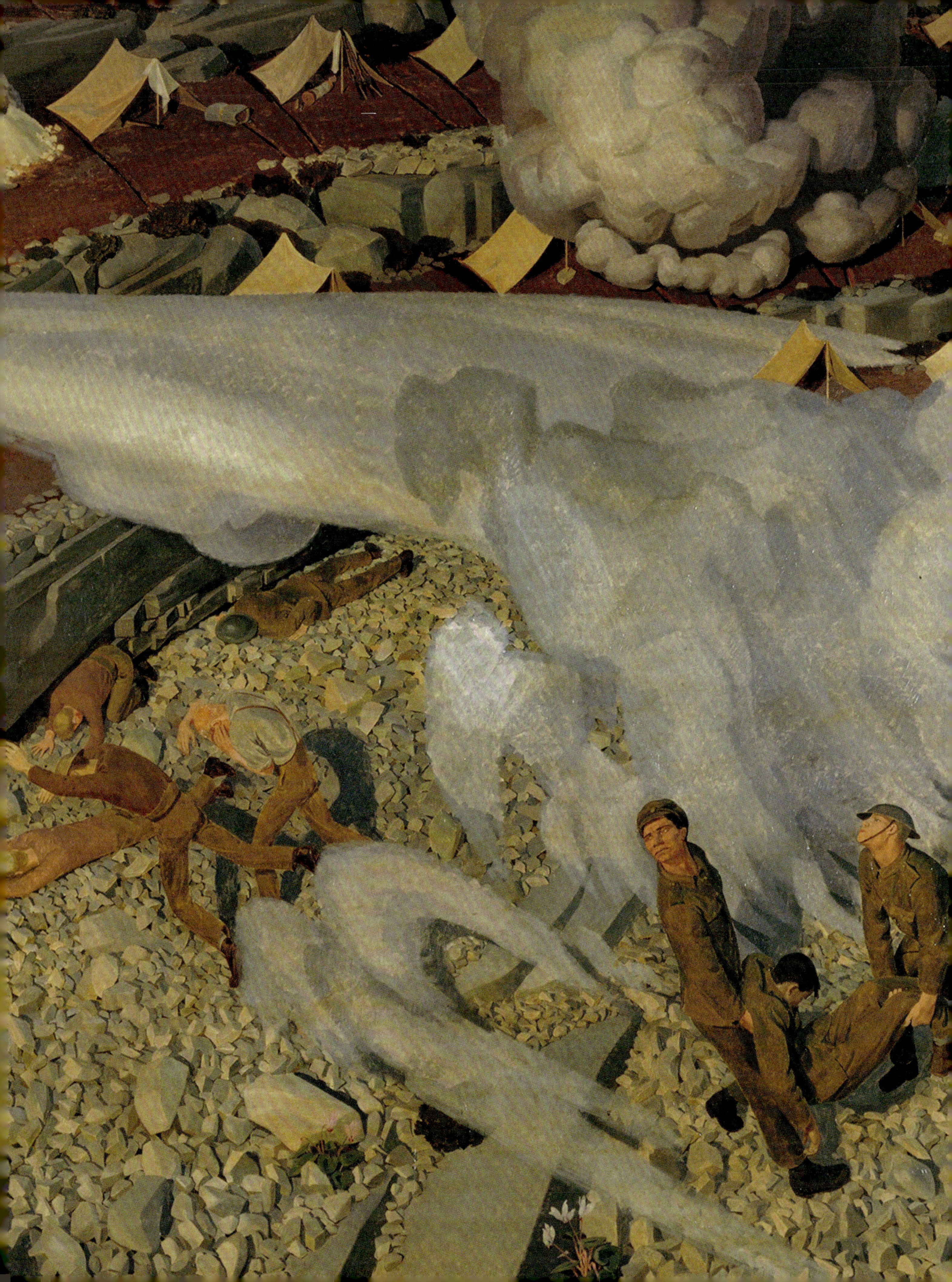

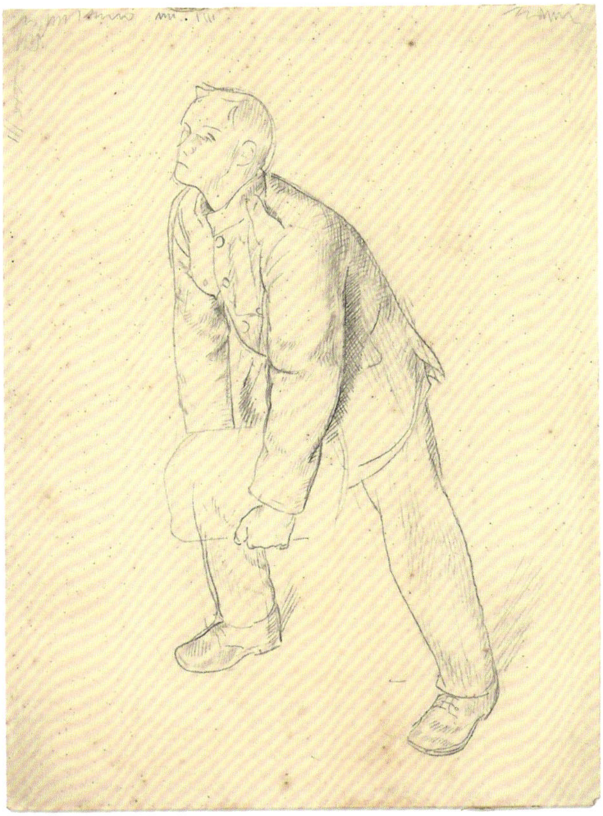

FIG. 13
Study for *Irish Troops*, c.1919
Pencil on paper, 305 × 230 mm
The Henry Lamb Estate

Lamb executed, and is perhaps as dramatic as any work in the proposed scheme. The painting's high horizon and exaggerated foreground may have had a more lasting influence on Spencer than first supposed – its composition resembling the rows of tents in *The Camp of Karasuli*, the upper part of his great project at the Sandham Memorial Chapel in Burghclere (completed more than a decade later).

With well over a year between the dramatic events depicted in *Irish Troops* and the painting's completion (scarcely in time for its unveiling at the Royal Academy in December 1919), Lamb was forced to make a theatrical reconstruction of its events through extensive use of studio models. As the series of studies suggests, the parts of the picture's complex composition that gave the artist the most technical issues related to the perspective and accurate foreshortening of the figures gathered in the foreground. Such careful and detailed study-making was a feature of Lamb's most successful larger-scale compositions, from *Fisherfolk* to *The Kennedy Family* – works that, like this, were required to be built up through an extensive period in the studio. No aspect of the artist's attempt to record accurate detail was left unaddressed. In a study showing one of the medics removing an injured soldier, Lamb recreated the physical effect of carrying an unresponsive body by having his model heave a heavily laden sack (fig. 13).

15

My Bivvy, 1920s

Oil on panel, 25.5 × 34 cm
Private collection

Lamb's ideas for pictures based on his experiences in the First World War would extend well into the early part of the 1920s. Alongside his monumental subject paintings like *Irish Troops* (cat. 14) and *Advance Dressing Station* (Manchester Art Gallery), Lamb would conceive of more mundane, even intimate compositions from his wartime memories. No works illustrate this better than the paintings *The Bivvy, Palestine* and the present, smaller version, *My Bivvy*. The picture was based on his time in Palestine in 1918 but not painted until 1923. Lamb also made numerous preparatory drawings for the composition in his sketchbooks. A characteristically awkward but strikingly original composition, *My Bivvy* shows Lamb himself (to the left) with two of his friends and fellow officers, Verschoyle and McWilliam, in their 'bivvy', or tent. This is apparently the first appearance of a favourite Lamb device when executing self-portraits within group paintings: the artist is shown turning his head away from the viewer and into the composition. It is a device that he would employ in two significant later paintings, *The Tea Party* (1926, cat. 27) and *The Artist's Family* (1940–43, Tate). The picture illustrates an event in Lamb's time in Palestine when he would be accused of drunkenness by his commanding officer – the narrative evoked through the wine bottles at the sitters' feet and the mug they appear to share at the centre of the work. The subject pre-dates Stanley Spencer's murals at the Sandham Memorial Chapel, sharing with those works an interest in capturing those humdrum moments of army life beyond the drama of the battlefield.

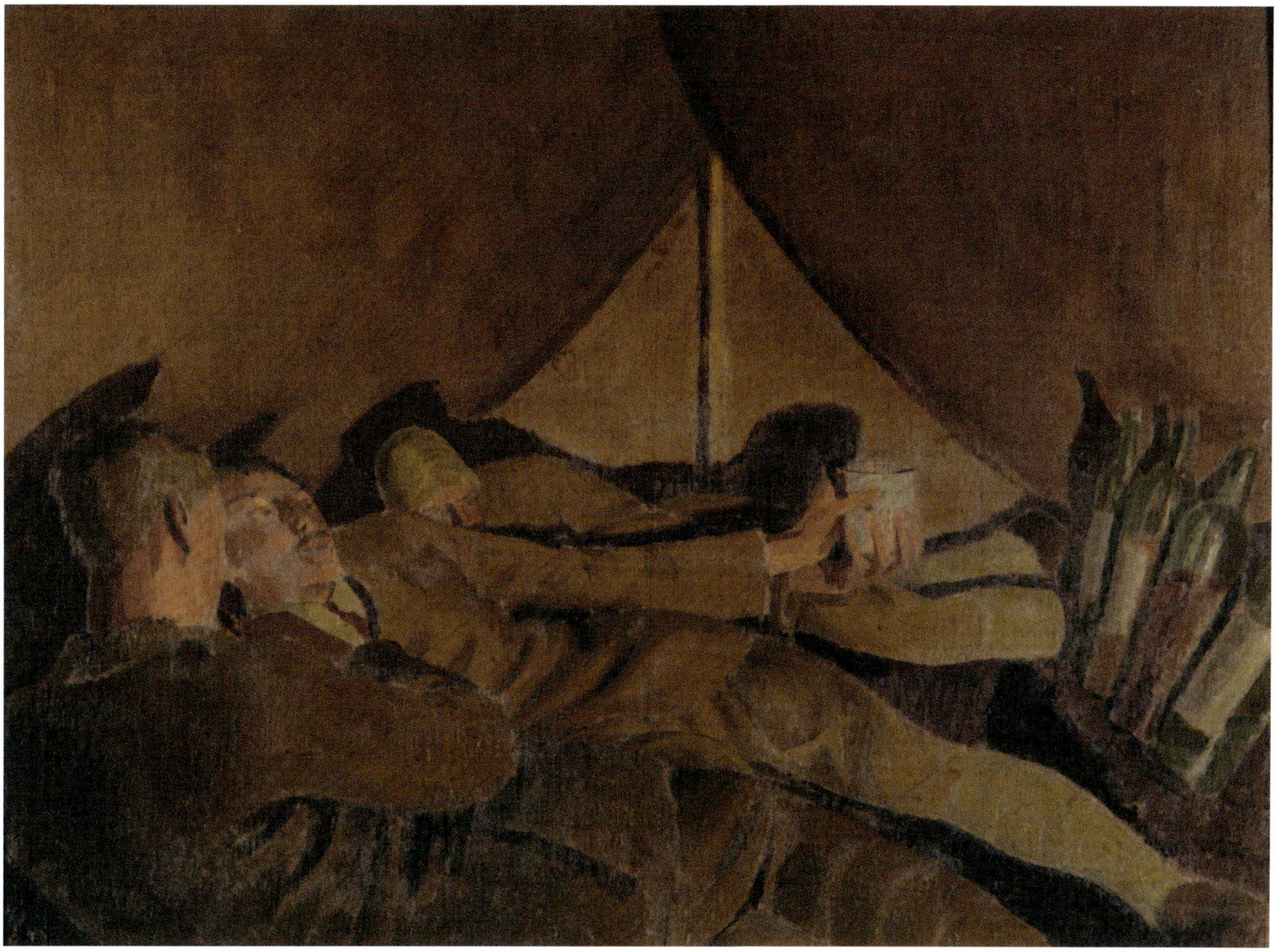

16

The P.B.I., 1941

Oil on canvas, 45.7 × 35.5 cm
Imperial War Museums

17

An Instructor at the Army and Royal Air Force Co-Operation School, 1941

Oil on canvas, 71 × 60.9 cm
Imperial War Museums

18

The Dispatch Rider, 1941

Oil on canvas, 59.5 × 49.5 cm
The Russell-Cotes Art Gallery & Museum, Bournemouth

Lamb's characteristically subdued, almost monochrome palette proves particularly effective in this rain-drenched military scene showing infantry troops making their way along a road after heavy rain (cat. 16). In its title Lamb deploys the well-known term for the 'Tommy' or infantryman – 'Poor Bloody Infantry'. The acronym was popularized in unofficial writing from the First World War, such as that found in the trench magazine *The Wipers Times*. As well as a reference to Lamb's own experiences in a war in which he had participated, it is evidence of a veiled respect for the junior soldier, one which pervades much of his most successful (and certainly heartfelt) work from the Second World War.

It was perhaps hardly surprising that Lamb, by now one of the country's most in-demand portraitists, would find that part of his official role as a war artist was to paint portraits of the military great and good. It was a task he took to at times reluctantly and with little love for his subject. As with *The Doler* (cat. 26) or his family's gardener at Coombe Bissett (cat. 38), his finest works in this genre were frequently his depictions of less obviously distinguished sitters. Two of the most successful works in this vein are *An Instructor at the Army and Royal Air Force Co-Operation School* (cat. 17) and *The Dispatch Rider* (cat. 18). Although the sitter in the latter has been possibly identified as Lance Corporal Fred Kennett of 225 Field Company, Lamb's titles indicate that he has chosen to anonymize his subjects so as to focus on the essence of his sitters' character and their role in the war effort. If Lamb's portraits from his time working for the WAAC have been criticized for being mundane, this is perhaps a fairer comment on his generals than on his foot soldiers. Works like these represent the fine character-studies that Lamb's best portraits are, subtly conveying the warmth and humanity of his sitter's character beyond the uniform (*An Instructor*) or their elements of awkwardness and vulnerability in their dedication to duty (*The Dispatch Rider*).

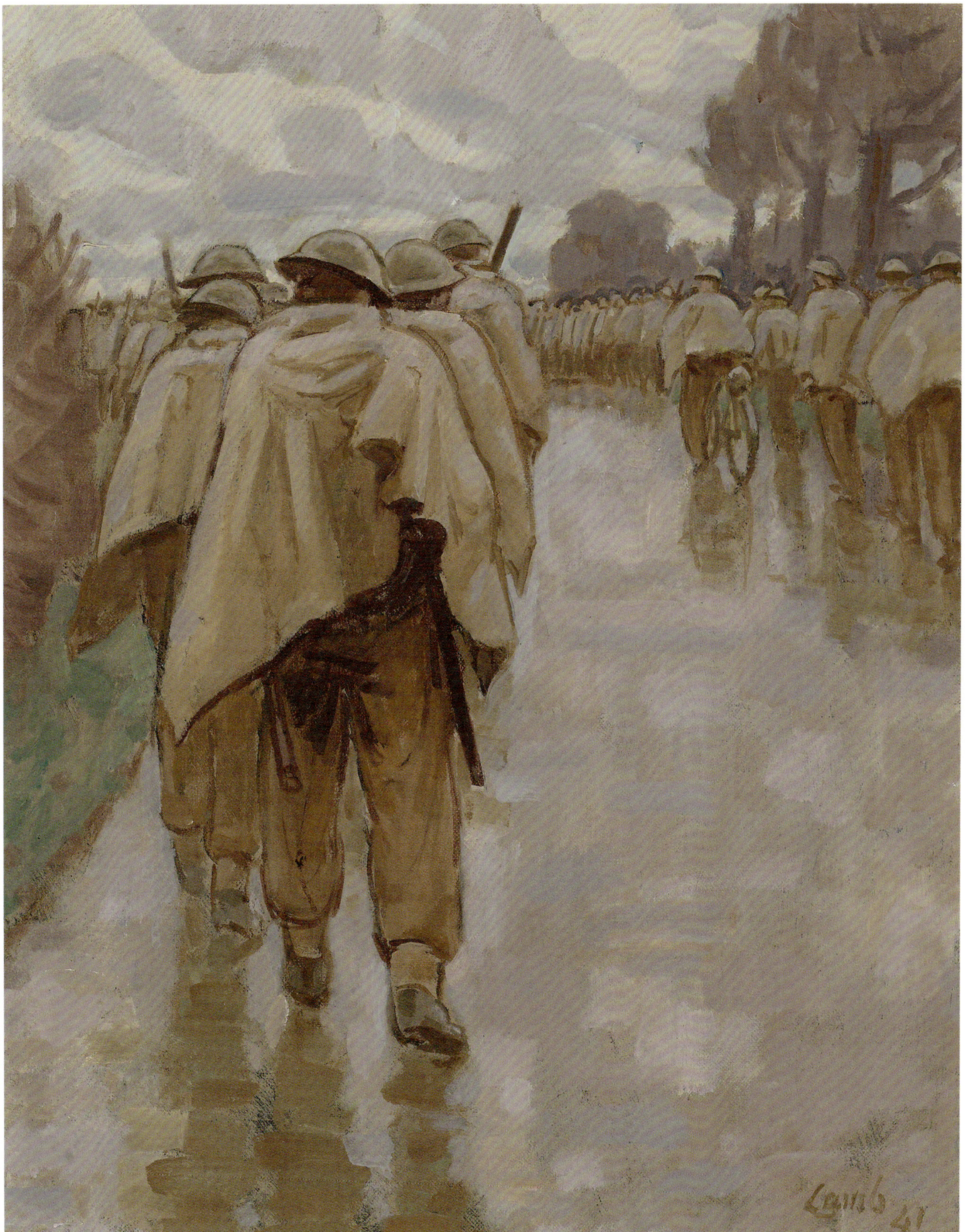
Lamb 41

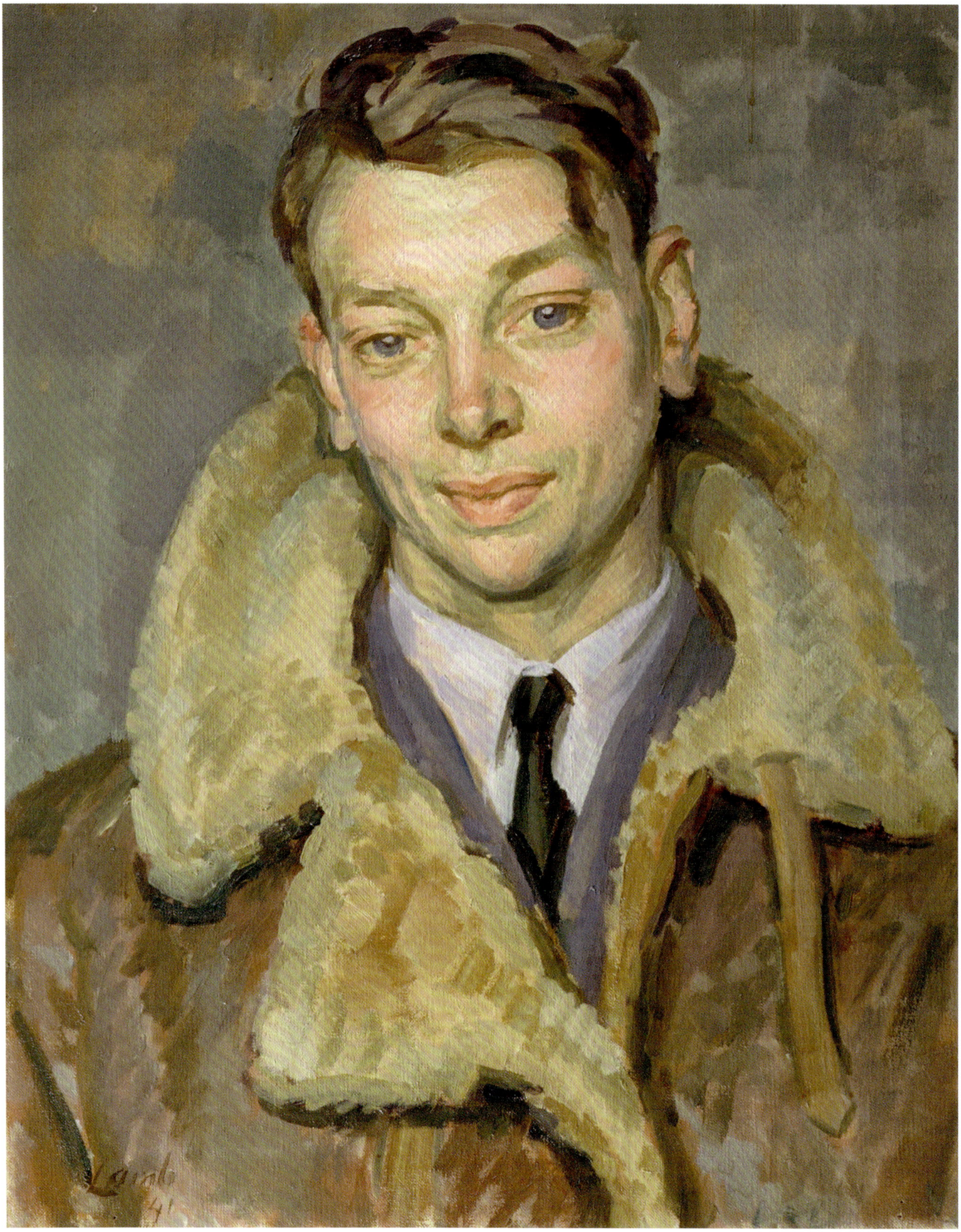

17

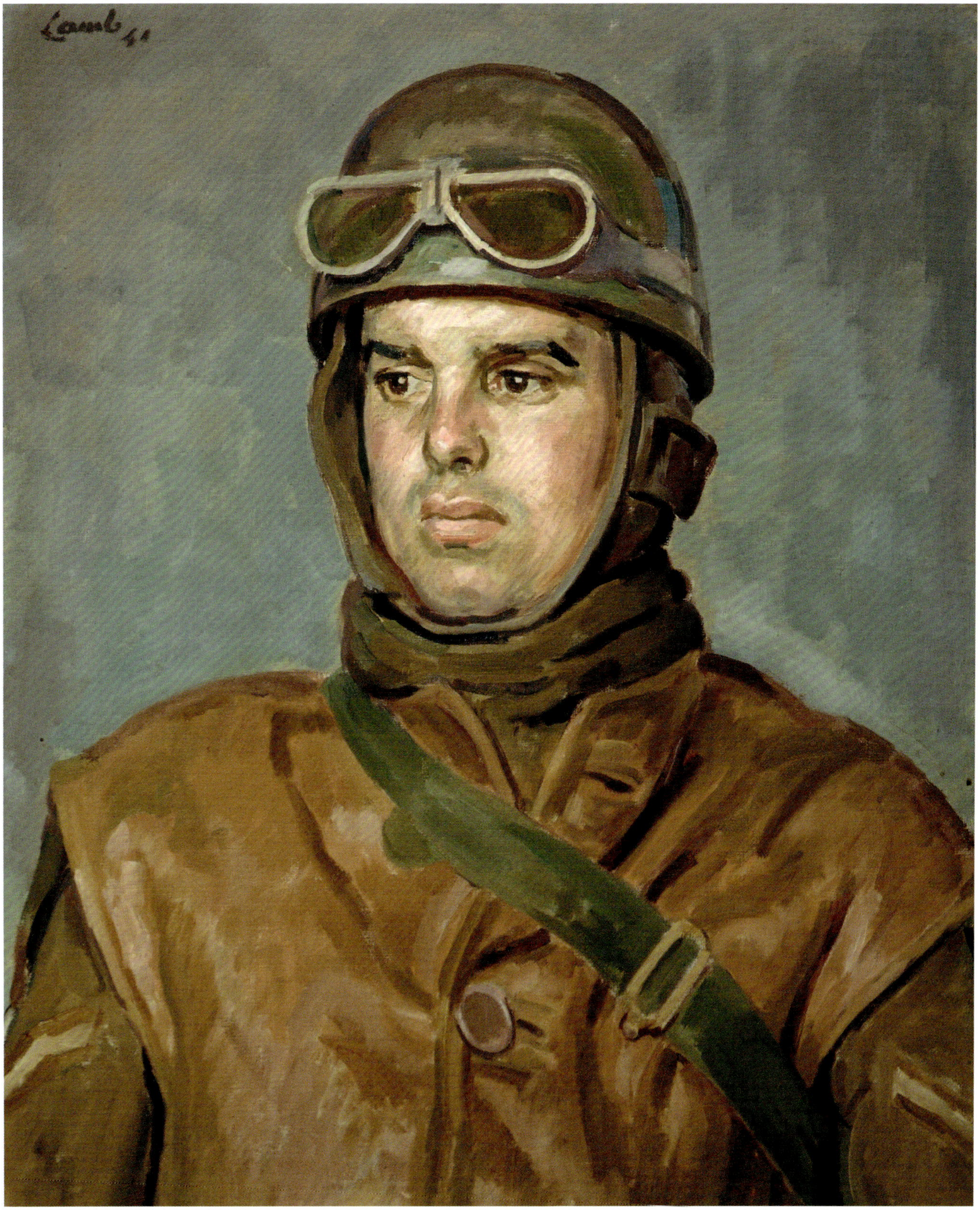

19

Pay Week at the Clothing Store, 1940

Oil on panel, 41.2 × 48.2 cm
Imperial War Museums

20

Canadian Troops Undergoing Instruction, 1942

Oil on canvas, 40.6 × 60.9 cm
Imperial War Museums

21

Page from a sketchbook of Second World War subjects

Pencil on paper, 250 × 380 mm
The Henry Lamb Estate

22

The Overhaul, 1941

Oil on canvas, 50.8 × 60.9 cm
Imperial War Museums

Lamb's Second World War paintings have tended to suffer from an unfair press. He was 57 by the outbreak of the War and by now well beyond the age of conscription, safely settled as he was into the rural existence which Coombe Bissett afforded him. Nevertheless, his output as a war artist was substantial, with more than a hundred paintings and drawings made of servicemen between 1940 and 1942. But Lamb was also concerned with the authenticity of his painting, concerned to record events only as he could observe them, which, as he put it, 'can hardly come from within as they did in my pictures of the other war'. The most successful were genre subjects, lively and frequently humorous depictions of everyday army life that have been rightly compared to the illustrations of Edward Ardizzone, a painter who Lamb had observed in the early 1940s. Lamb would self-consciously adopt Ardizzone's approach to subject matter when addressing the issue of how best to depict a war of which he was but a distant observer. Beyond the portrait commission, Lamb would follow Stanley Spencer's example of recording the rudimentary and everyday, no more so than in perhaps one of earliest works of this type, *Pay Week at the Clothing Store* from 1940 (cat. 19). Elsewhere there is evidence of a serious interest in teaching himself technical aspects of his subject matter, in order, for instance, accurately to depict the military hardware he would encounter; his sketchbooks are full of tanks and of aircraft, such as the Westland Lysander monoplane (cat. 21). These would be developed into a work like *The Overhaul*, showing engineers at work on this very type of aircraft. Despite this, there is evidence that Lamb would gain little pleasure from such commissions. It was not until a meeting with the Canadian High Commissioner, Vincent Massey, in October 1941 that Lamb's spirits were raised. The work he produced with 12th Tank Division

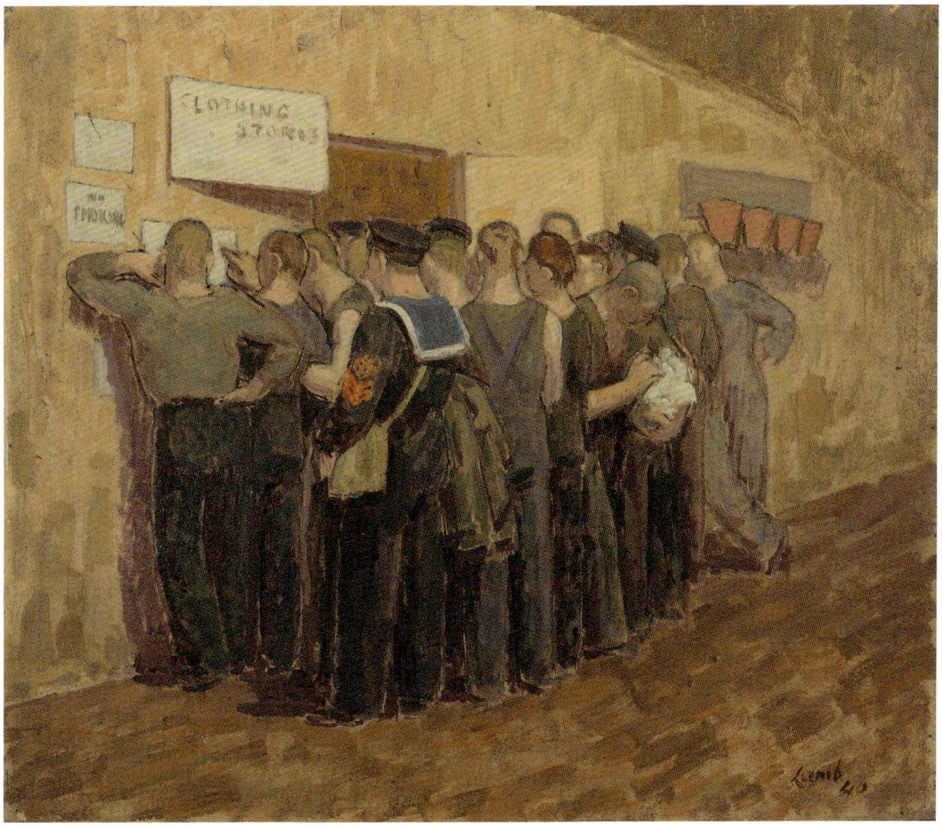

19

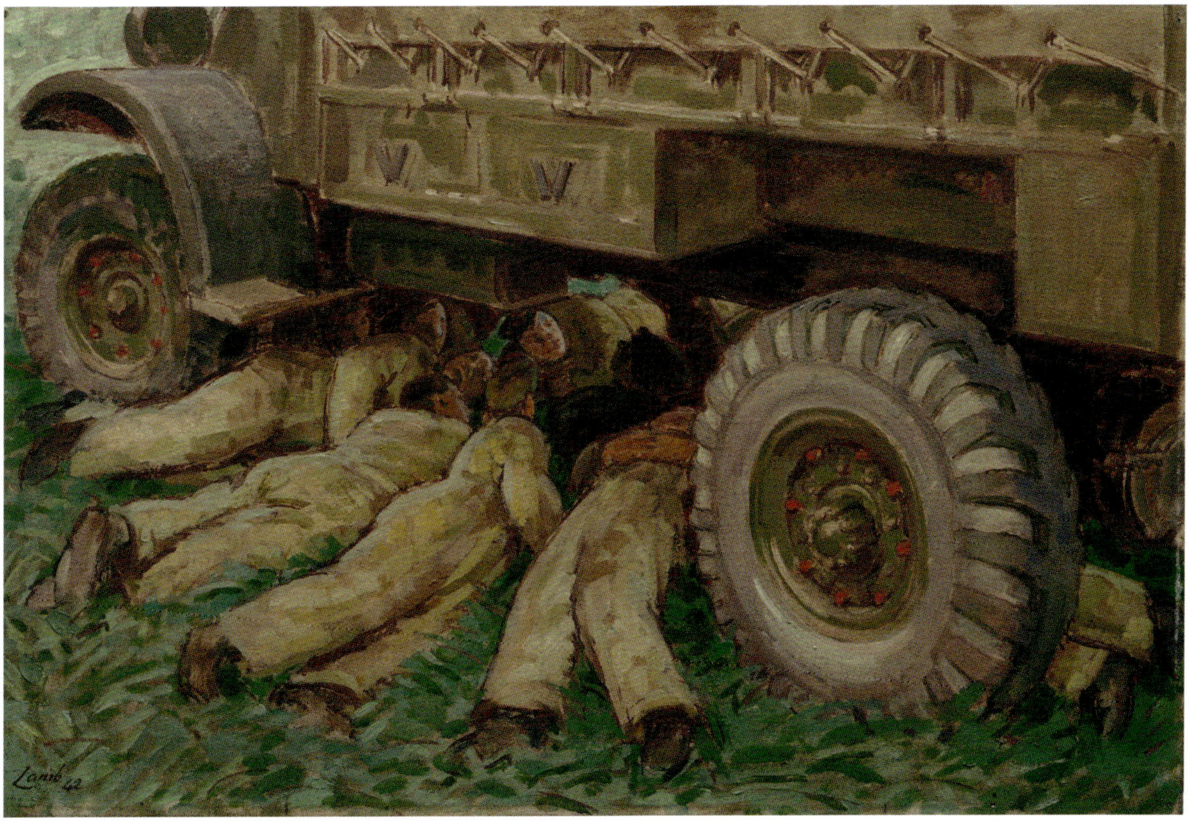

20

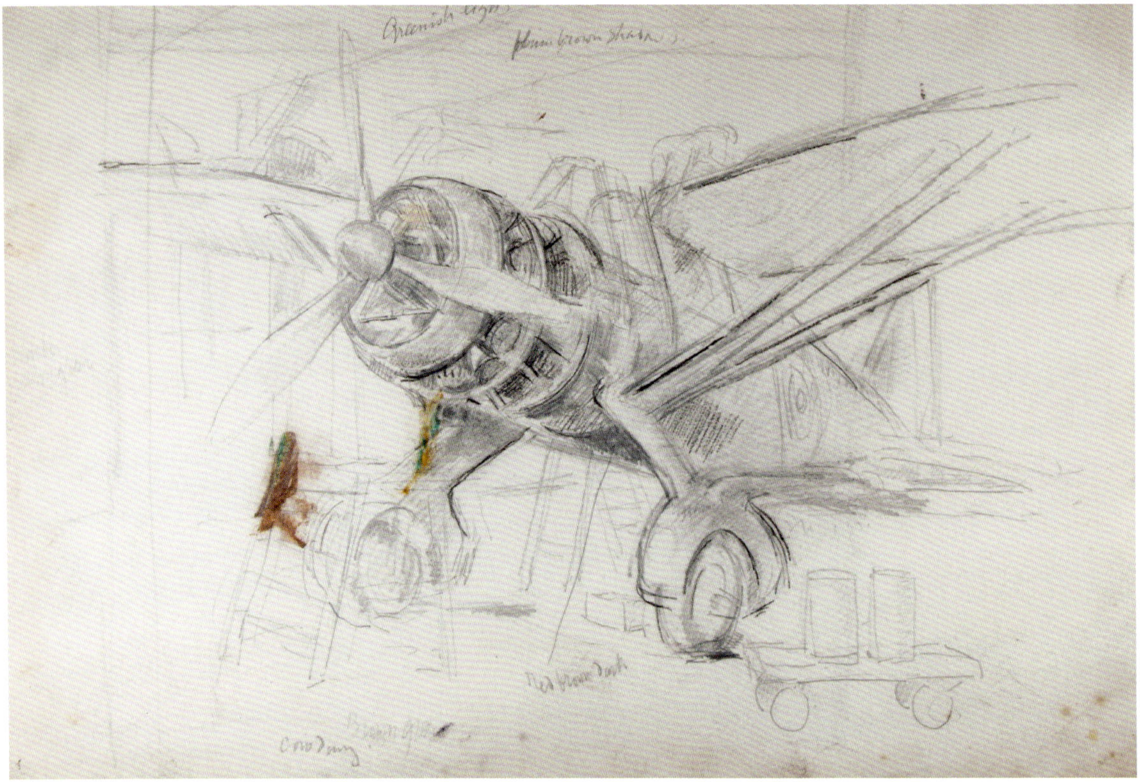

21

of the Canadian Army, late in 1941 and throughout much of 1942, is perhaps his most successful of the entire war. Here, finally inspired by his surroundings (claiming there was 'nothing more lovely in England' than the hills to the south of Thames Estuary) and perhaps more importantly the company of the Canadian troops, he produced pictures like *Canadian Troops Undergoing Instruction* (cat. 20) and *Canadian Troops Replacing Tracks* (Canadian War Museum, Ottawa), works full of lively detail and inventive humour. Although undoubtedly comparable to Ardizzone's, they must also seen in the context of Lamb's own painting, particularly his figure scenes from the 1930s and trademark larger-scale conversation pieces such as *Evening in the Village* from back in 1935 (cat. 40).

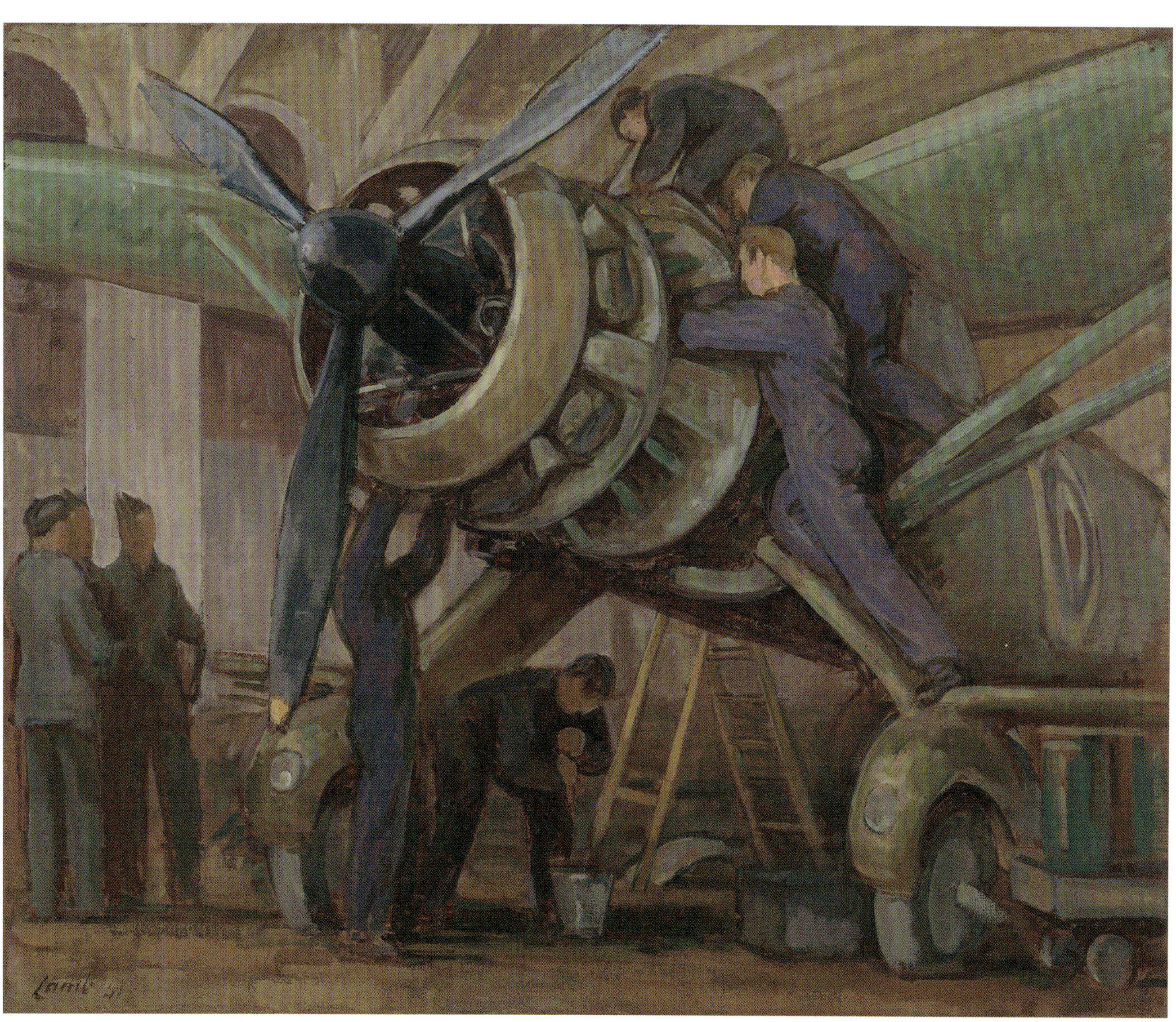

FRIENDS AND RELATIONSHIPS, POOLE PERIOD

23

Paradise Street, 1923

Oil on canvas, 49 × 62.5 cm
Poole Museum (Purchased from Spink & Co., with the assistance of the Victoria and Albert Museum Purchase Grant Fund, 1984)

Lamb first visited the Dorset coast with Lady Ottoline Morrell in 1911, then in a further trip in 1912 with Lytton Strachey in which he was particularly struck by the beauty of Lulworth Cove and Cerne Abbas.[1] By 1922, having been living in the Dorset countryside (at Stourpaine), he alighted on the harbour town of Poole, where he acquired his first house, No. 10 Hill Street. Poole's lure to Lamb – even if secondary to its proximity to the Johns at Alderney Manor – must have been its position as a thriving, working harbour town. Its working-class population may also have appealed to him, in much the same way as the Breton peasant world of Doëlan or the weather-beaten toughness of Gola Island had. A constant artistic appeal to Lamb revealed itself in the architecture of the harbour itself, its thin streets and high warehouse buildings. This backdrop enabled him to indulge his artistic eye for unusual viewpoints and vistas, executing a series of remarkable street scenes which remain amongst his most successful non-portrait-based works.

Paradise Street depicts the narrow street lined with warehouses that leads from the High Street and emerges on to the quayside. The pub 'The Kings Arms' (today 'The Stable Restaurant') faces the viewer on the left of the picture. On the right is a warehouse that is now Poole Museum and the Library, which functioned then as a gymnasium under the aegis of Lady Wimbourne.[2] As a composition it is one of Lamb's most successful. Something in these views awoke his nascent 'Camden Townism', allowing him to stand back and observe the bustling energy of harbour life in a way that has even been compared to Sickert's many depictions of the harbour at Dieppe.[3] With works like *Paradise Street*, Lamb, ever aware of the theatrical quality of architecture, played inventively with viewpoints, composition and contrasts of light and shade. As real as the streets depicted are, they retain something of a contrived quality that perfectly suited Lamb, the studio painter.

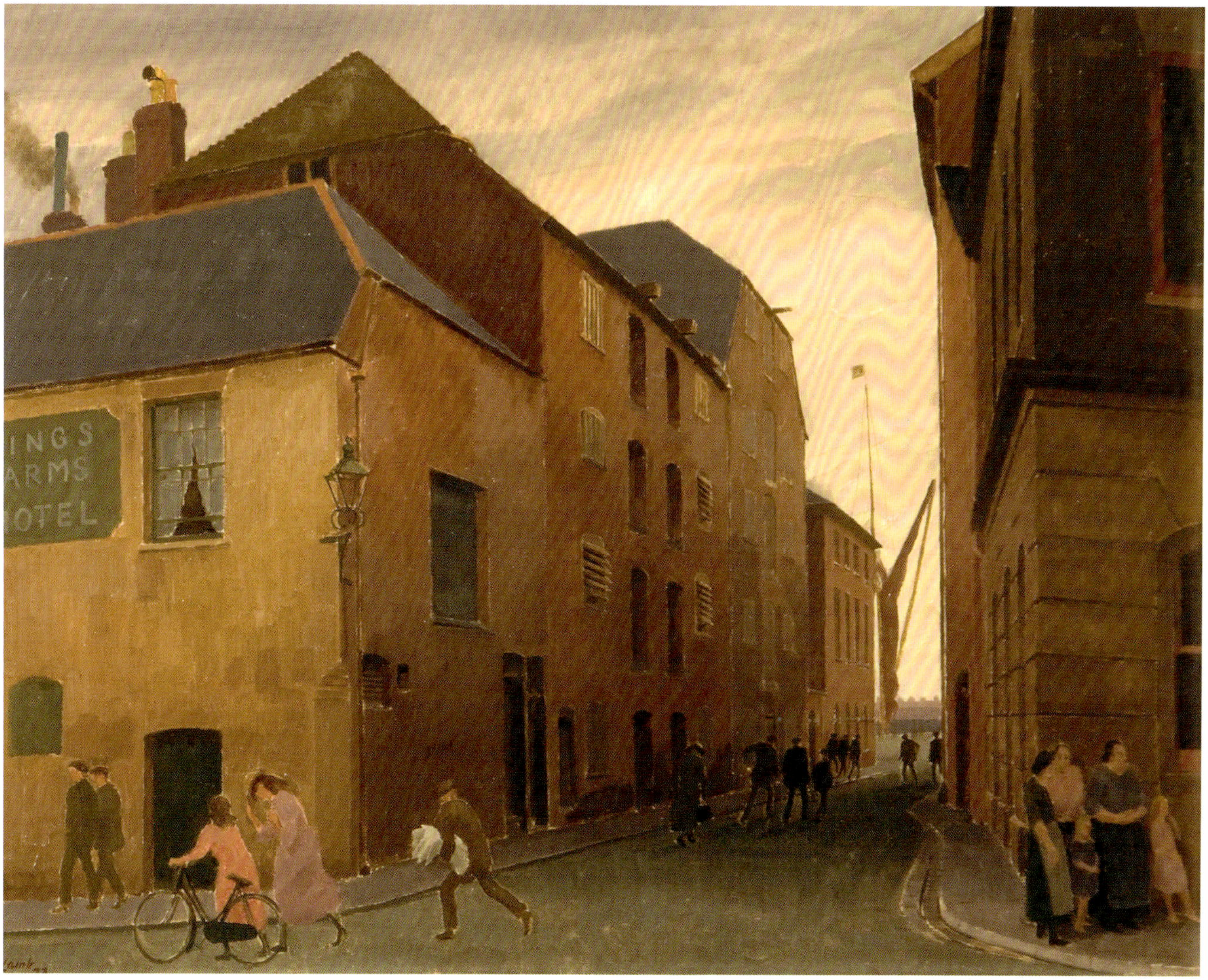
INGS
ARMS
OTEL

24

View from the Artist's Studio, Poole, 1922

Oil on canvas, 49 × 39.5 cm
Private collection

Many of Lamb's most successful Poole street scenes were painted in fairly quick succession following his move to the town in 1922. Frequently critical of own work, Lamb appears to have held these pictures in high regard, writing to Richard Carline: 'I have finished two roof views from the windows of my stable and I think their quality is better than those green landscapes I did last summer'.[4] *View From the Artist's Studio, Poole,* also known as *The Coffin Shop* (probably one of these 'roof views') is notable in being devoid of any human element. It was painted from the first floor of Lamb's Hill Street home, with the barn studio visible at the end of the garden. Behind this is the roofline of buildings that still exist today at the junction of Market Cross and Dear Hay Lane. The source of the work's title is to be found in the prominent building in the centre of the picture, identified by Peter Davies as 'an oddly shaped building used by Mr Cole, the undertaker'.[5] Despite the work's rich but monochrome colouring and lack of activity, it is one of Lamb's most satisfying townscapes, the scene greatly enhanced by the washing line that dominates much of the lower right hand section of the picture. It is a device that is reminiscent of Stanley Spencer. This influence is regularly cited in Lamb's Poole paintings, a particular source being identified in the steep roofline of an early work by Spencer, *Mending Cowls, Cookham* from 1914, a complete sketch of which appears in a letter from Spencer to Lamb. This was painted nearly ten years earlier, however, and it is equally instructive to look at works from the same period such as *Christ Carrying the Cross* (1920) and *Christ Healing a Paralytic* (c.1920), both evidence of a similarly theatrical use of buildings in Spencer's work that perhaps points to the close relationship of the two artists at the time. A perhaps overlooked influence is Stanley's brother Gilbert Spencer. Lamb's *Feeding Calves* from the previous year (private collection) is uncannily close to many of Gilbert's rural subject paintings,[6] and something of his almost naïve simplicity is also evident in *View from the Artist's Studio*. Lamb's Poole street scenes appear to have been an almost immediate success amongst the artist's followers, with George Kennedy illustrating no fewer than four of them amongst the relatively small number of plates selected for his monograph on Lamb in 1924.

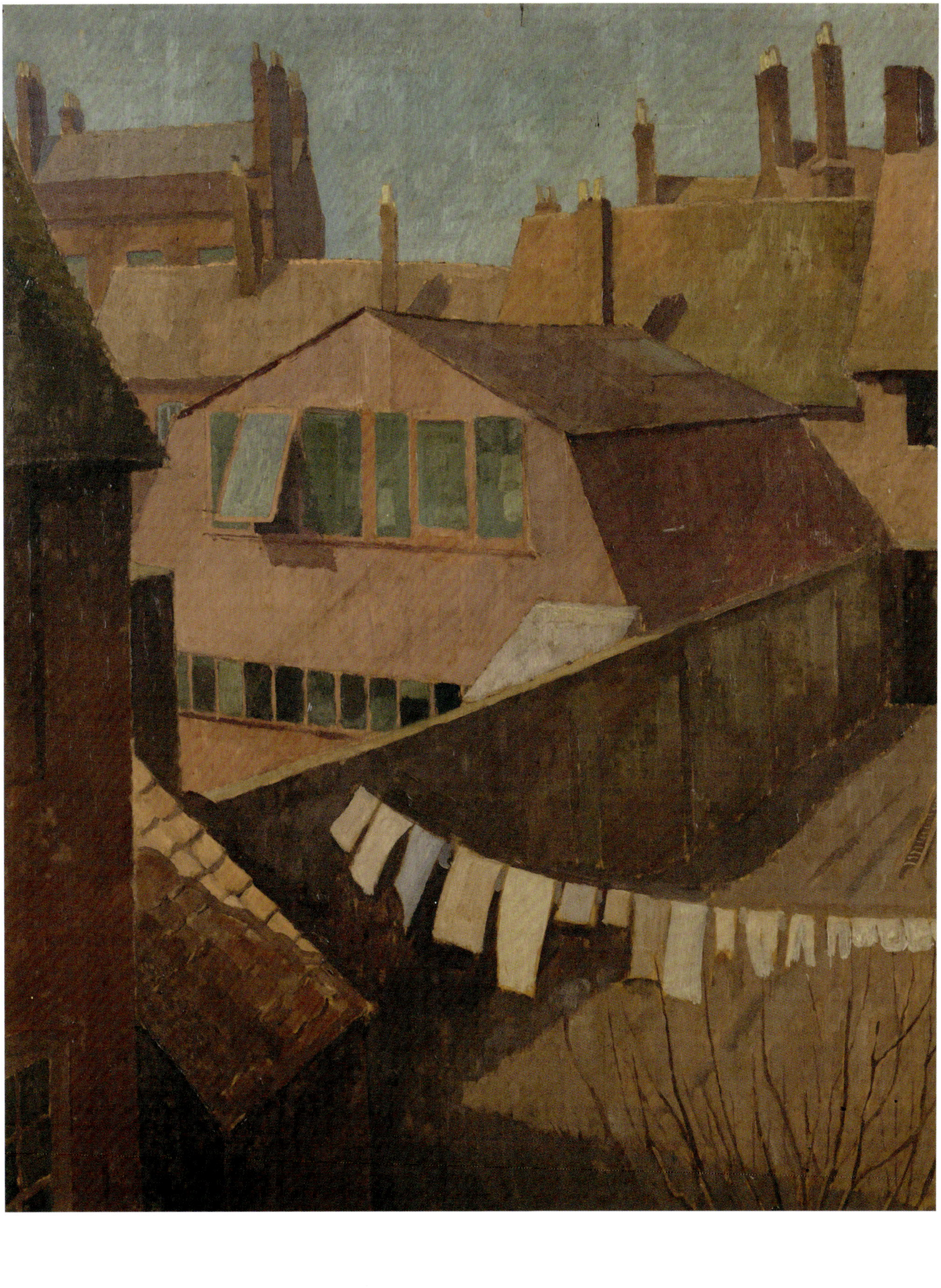

25

A Street in Poole, Dorset, 1922

Oil on panel, 23 × 28 cm
Poole Museum (Purchased in 1986 with the support of the Art Fund)

It has been suggested that this small street scene shows houses on Lagland Street in Poole.[7] The scale and fresh *alla prima* style of execution and tone, particularly in the brooding approach of the evening sky, is suggestive of a *plein air* method that is rare in Lamb's work of this era. The work is animated by its figurative element, the triple grouping of figures to the centre almost recalling Augustus John's Equihen fisherfolk from the beginning of the century or the artist's own Gola Island women. A similar work, painted on board of a comparable width but longer length, *High Street, Poole* (Russell Cotes Art Gallery, Bournemouth) is even more spontaneous in its spirit of execution, and is an emptier study for the background of the more finished painting of the same title, *High Street, Poole* of 1923 (private collection).

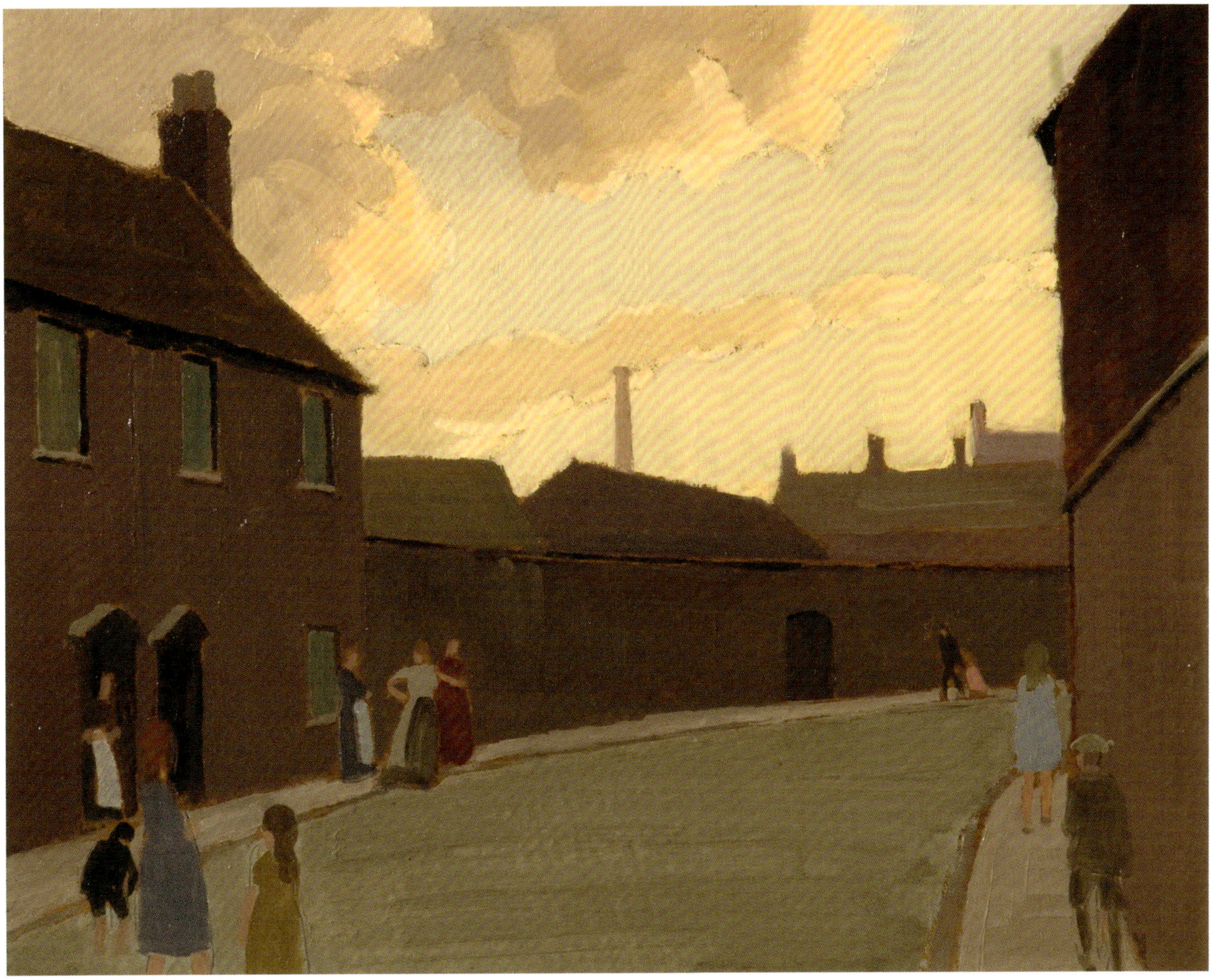

26

The Doler, 1922

Oil on canvas, 49 × 39 cm
Poole Museum (Purchased from Thomas Agnew & Sons Ltd
with the assistance of the National Art Collections Fund, 1989)

The Doler, deliberately unidentified by the artist, could be seen as a symbol of the depressed reality and high unemployment Lamb found on his arrival in Poole. The sitter is said to have first encountered Lamb when haranguing him outside his Hill Street home, throwing stones at the window and railing against him for his perceived privileged, work-shy existence.[8] Although six years later Lamb would marry into the Anglo-Irish aristocracy, he was often motivated by a degree of inverse snobbery in his favoured choice of subject. With this direct character study Lamb succeeds in both capturing the essence of his sitter and representing a type, as he did with other memorable, anonymous portraits, from *Breton Youth* (cat. 3) to *The Dispatch Driver* (cat. 18).

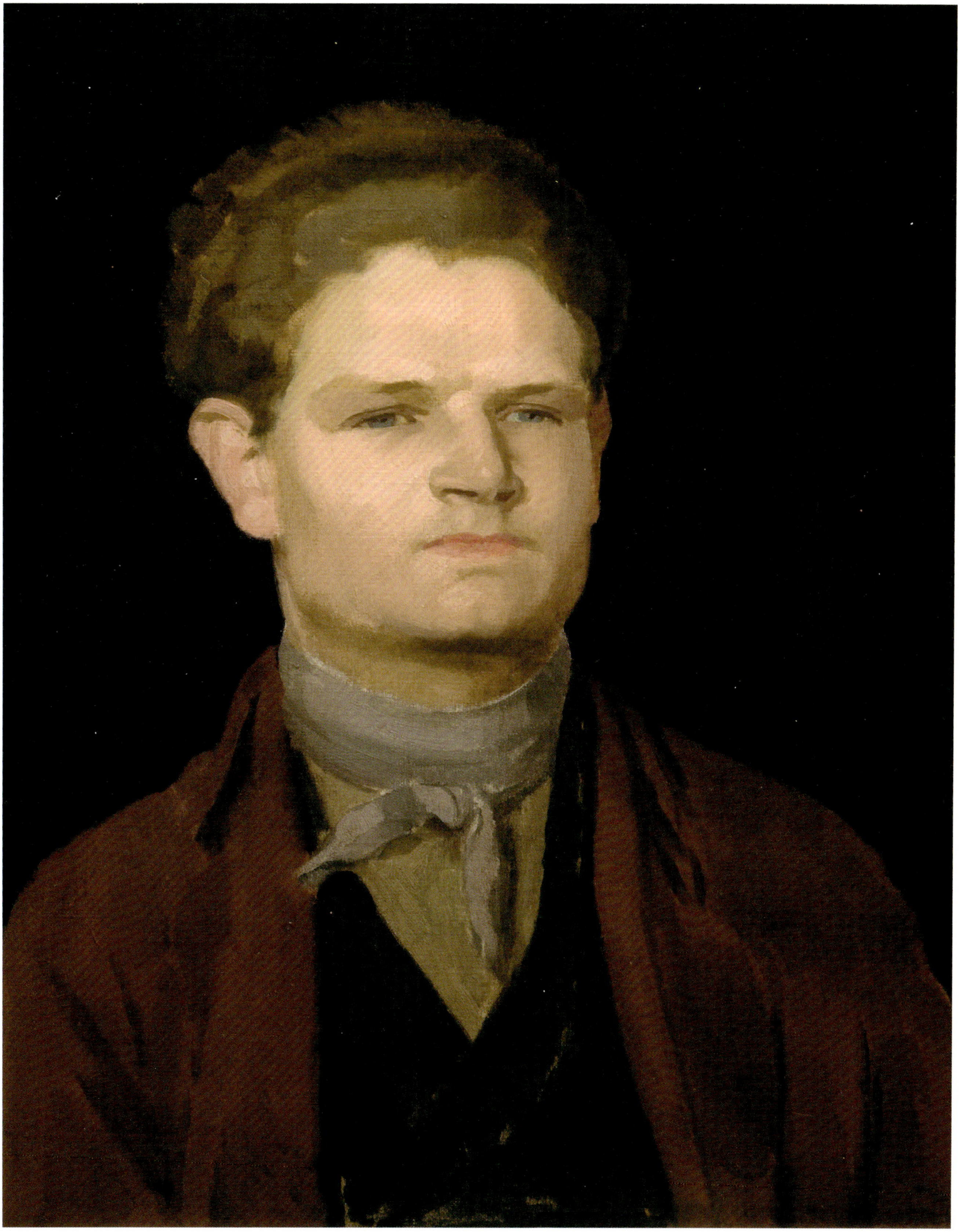

27

The Tea Party (or The Round Table), 1926

Oil on canvas, 184.6 × 143.6 cm
Private collection
POOLE ONLY

Also known by the title *The Round Table*, the present work is one of Lamb's most ambitious, complex and monumental conversation pieces. It depicts the artist's living room at No. 10 Hill Street, looking through its elegant bay window into the gardens beyond. The identity of each of the work's sitters has only been firmly established relatively recently. The central focus of the work is Stanley Spencer, who, seated to the upper right of the table, waxes lyrical to a captivated audience of Lamb's guests. The couple to Spencer's left have been recently confirmed as the artist's Poole neighbours Mr and Mrs Ernest Edenden, a coal merchant and his wife who would go on to buy No. 10 from Lamb in 1928.[9] Contemporary photographs confirm the single male figure to Spencer's right as the businessman and politician Frederick Leverton Harris. More significantly, Harris was also an amateur painter and collector. In the previous year he had held a show of his work at the Goupil Gallery just prior to Spencer's own one-man exhibition there in 1926. Harris also owned at least two works by Spencer that subsequently entered public collections – one of which, *The Poultry Market, Petersfield*, also painted in 1926 and now in the Government Art Collection, can, intriguingly, be compared to some of Lamb's Poole street views from the earlier 1920s. One can safely assume that Harris, who died the year this painting was completed, attended the tea party as an acolyte and admirer of Spencer and his work. Lamb himself is seated with his back to the viewer at the bottom of the picture.

Lamb's inspiration for this picture can probably be traced to another Stanley Spencer-centred painting, *Gathering on the Terrace at 47 Downshire Hill, Hampstead*, from 1924–25, by his close friend Richard Carline. Lamb's letters to Carline suggest he took it upon himself to act as advisor on the work's awkward composition, in which Lamb himself was a sitter. *The Tea Party* is also one of Lamb's most psychologically complex and layered works – symptomatic of the lonely and isolated state he found himself in towards the end of the 1920s. Central to this is the table itself,[10] exaggerated and elongated, as if viewed slightly from above and depicted as if to suggest a huge distance between the work's sitters. No less significant is the distance that is cast between Spencer and Lamb. Since before the First World War, the two painters had enjoyed a long association, which by the mid 1920s, partly owing to Spencer's prolonged periods as Lamb's house guest at Hill Street, was beginning to sour. Letters suggest Lamb was growing tired of Spencer's company.[11] The extent to which *The Tea Party* is redolent of Lamb's own feeling of isolation is heightened by the artist's decision to depict himself facing away from the viewer.

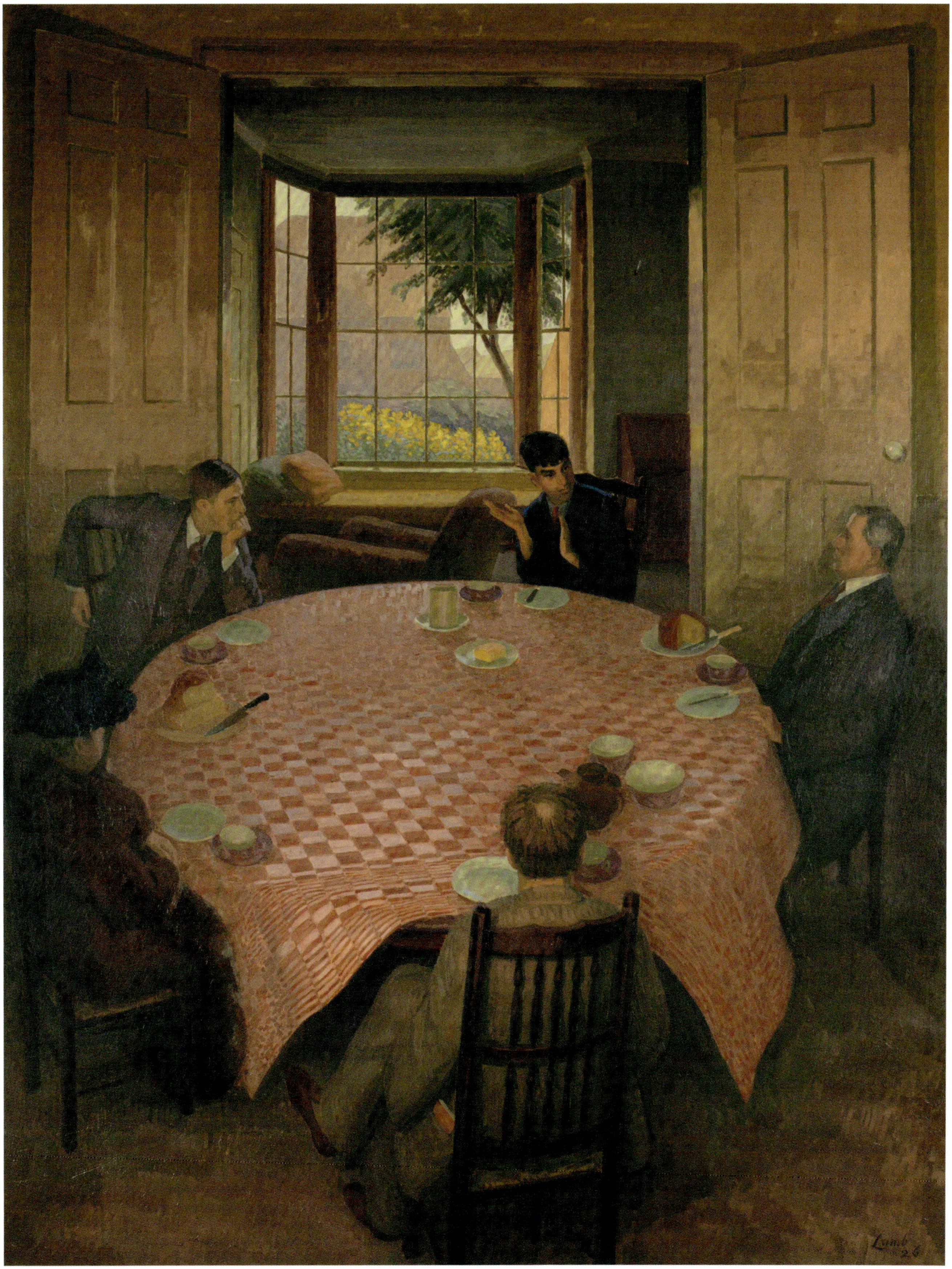
Lamb 26

28

Tall Trees near Alderney Manor, Dorset, before 1928

Oil on panel, 22.4 × 31.1 cm
Poole Museum

Augustus John's biographer Michael Holroyd has described Alderney Manor as 'a strange fortified bungalow, larger than most houses, which had been built by an eccentric Frenchman'.[12] The house, set in 60 acres near Parkstone on the edge of Poole in Dorset, was rented by the John family for £50 a year from 1911. Lamb was evidently captivated by the place and the John family's carefree existence there, waxing lyrical about its atmosphere in a letter to Lytton Strachey just prior to his second visit to Brittany in 1911. When Lamb arrived in Poole in the early 1920s he remained a regular visitor, and the present landscape apparently depicts an unidentified avenue of trees somewhere in the vicinity of the house. The picture was formerly in the possession of Lamb's (and subsequently Spencer's) great patrons Mary and Louis Behrend. The inscription on the reverse (presumably in Mary Behrend's hand) proposes a date before 1928, plausible not only on the basis of style but also given that the Johns had left Alderney Manor in 1927, with Lamb moving to Coombe Bissett a year later. A compositional pencil sketch for the painting is in the collection of the artist's family.

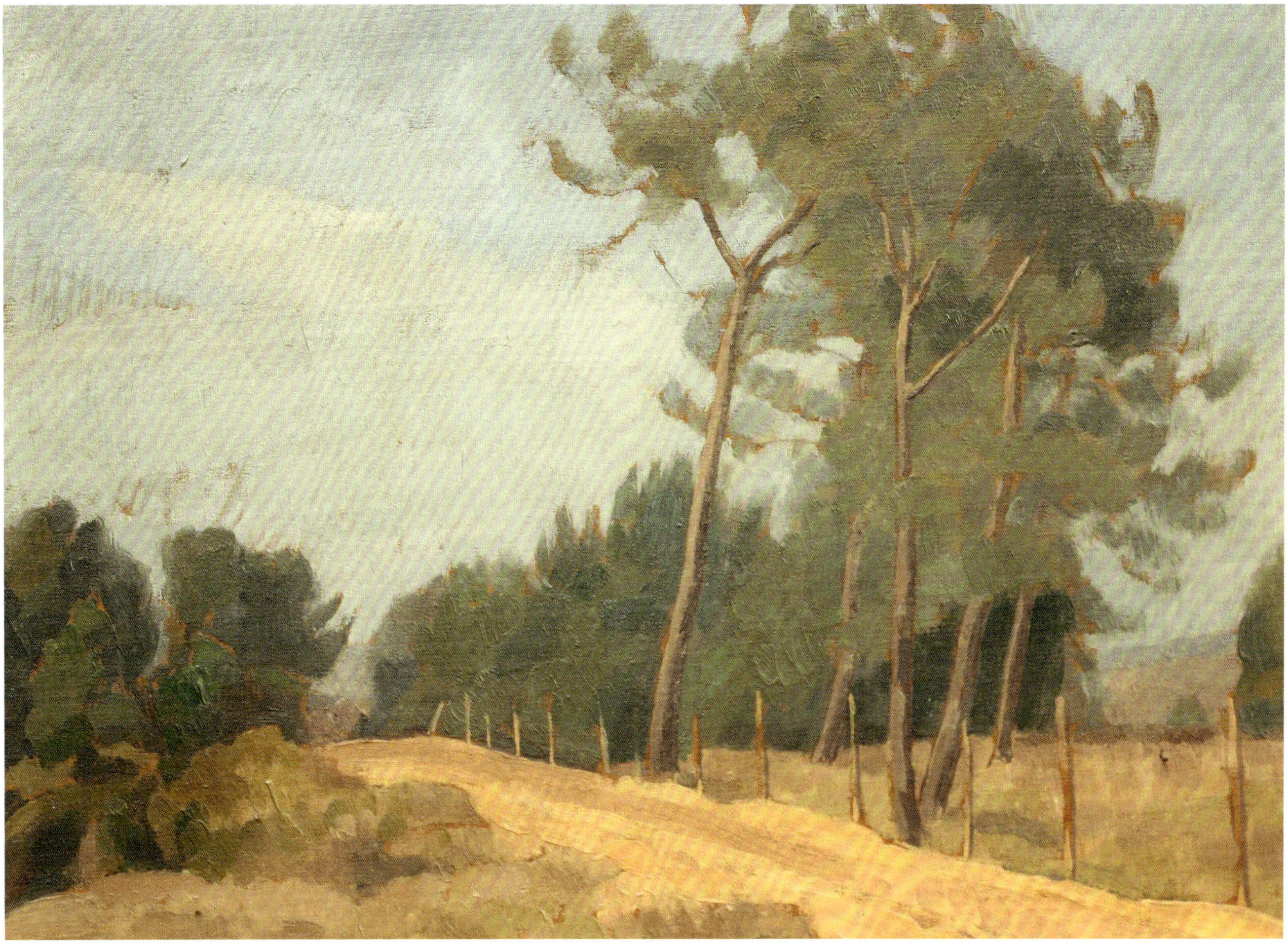

29

Study for *The Anrep Family*, c.1919

Watercolour over pen and ink on paper, 165 × 238 mm
Private collection

The Anrep Family is the first of Lamb's major family portrait groups from the early 1920s. These compositionally highly complex works would be some of the most successful portraits he would ever produce, offering insights not just into the personalities of each of his sitters but also into the subtleties of each family's dynamic. Lamb had first met Boris Anrep while the two studied at the Académie Julian in Paris in 1908. According to Keith Clements, Lady Ottoline Morrell described Anrep as 'clever, fat, good-hearted, sensual ... full of youthful vitality and Russian gaiety'.[13] Anrep would become one of the foremost artists in mosaic of his generation, executing large schemes in the medium at the National Gallery in London and at Westminster Cathedral. Through Dorelia, Anrep met and fell in love with Helen Maitland. They lived together from 1911 and had two children, Anastasia and Igor, before eventually marrying in 1918. The marriage was not a happy one, and in 1925 Helen left Anrep to live with Roger Fry. The present work is an early sketch for the final painting, which was acquired by the Museum of Fine Arts in Boston in 1932. As a study it shows some notable differences from the final painting, the most intriguing of which would be the addition of a painting above above Boris's head from which a pair of legs can be seen and to the far right the appearance of the figure of Maroussa Volkova, Anrep's assistant and eventually mistress – ironically a significant factor in the break-up of the marriage. Also significant is the figure of Helen, who in the present work is depicted facing in as if to engage with Anrep. Perhaps rather tellingly in the final painting she appears more detached, facing away from her husband. Another later watercolour study (also in a private collection)[14] includes the family's dog to the far centre right of the composition. The dog also appears in an oil sketch for the portrait but was abandoned in the final painting.

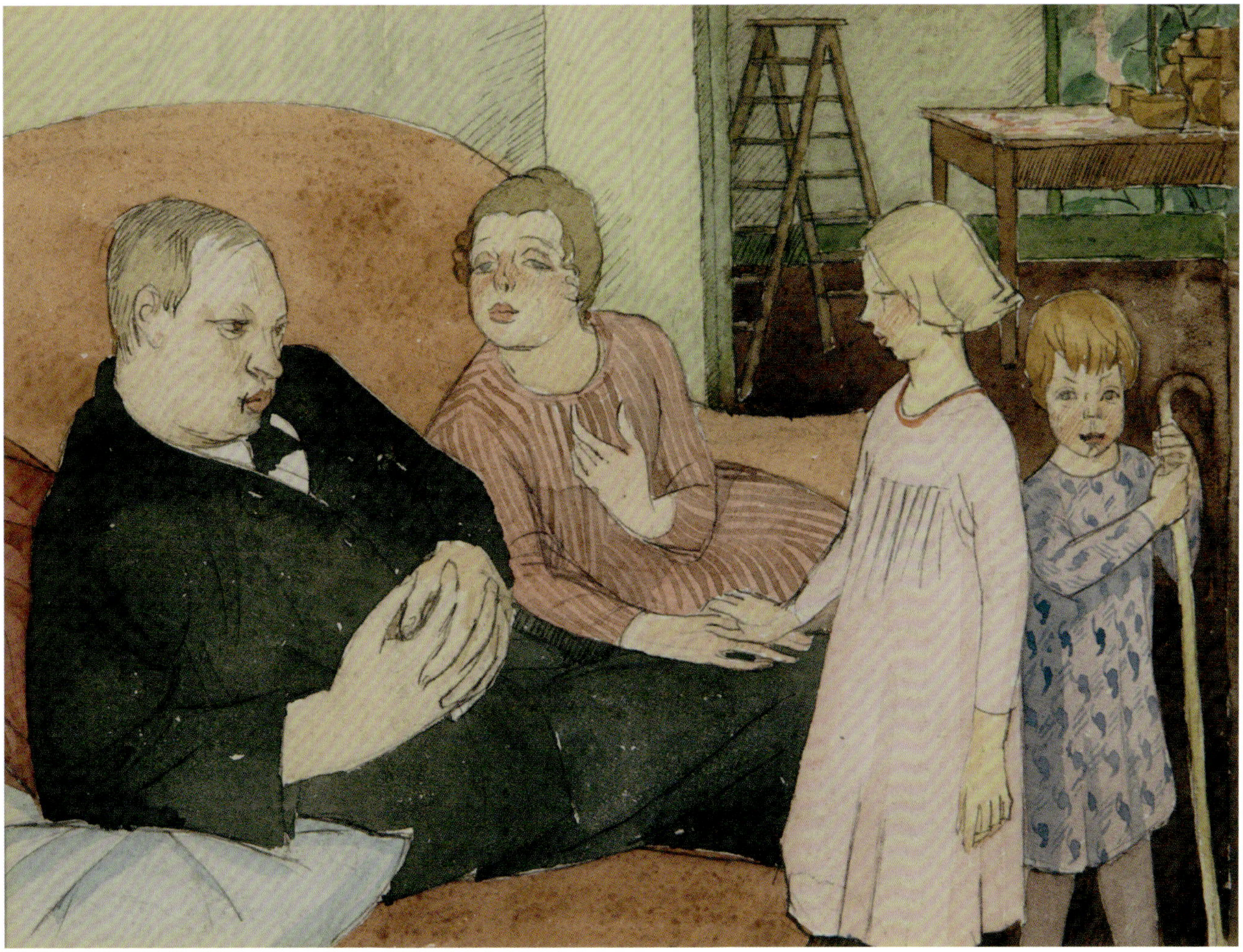

30

The Kennedy Family, 1921

Oil on canvas, 112.8 × 82.1 cm
Private collection

In the early part of his life Lamb had few more loyal friends than George Kennedy, the artist turned architect who he had first met while Kennedy was studying at the Académic Julian in Paris in 1906. An admirer and constant (if not always reliable) critic of Lamb's work, he wrote in 1924 the only monograph on Henry Lamb published in the artist's lifetime. It was Kennedy who encouraged Lamb to travel to Ireland in 1912 on a journey that would result in his great Gola Island paintings. He also accompanied Lamb to Fécamp in 1915, having the humility to take on the role of his orderly. *The Kennedy Family* is the second of Lamb's great family portrait groups, after the Anreps. Like many of the artist's conversation pieces, it was painstakingly developed through a large body of detailed studies and a very accurate oil sketch, before being finished over time in the studio. Like *The Anrep Family* before it, the painting's success lies in its ungainliness. Unashamedly contrived through being pieced together from the many studio studies, this very awkwardness is the key to the picture's originality. It conveys elements both of realism, in the careful studies of each of the sitters' faces, and of impossibility, in the elongation and stylization of the drawing room interior and the anatomical exaggeration of the figures.

At various times the influence of Stanley Spencer has been cited in *The Kennedy Portrait*. But what portrait, let alone portrait group, by Spencer is comparable as early as 1921? As Lamb painted this work, Spencer was still emerging from the Giotto-esque naivety of his earlier style to the mature one of the later 1920s. Indeed, a number of works by Spencer from the following decade, including the quirkily awkward *Hilda, Unity and Dolls* of 1937 (Leeds Museum), could be said to owe a debt to *The Kennedy Family*. Kennedy himself would struggle to articulate his views on this most complex of compositions in the essay in his book on Lamb written only three years later: '... he seems to have realised more completely the limitations as well as the possibilities of this type of portraiture. The play of character it allows, and the kind of diffused consciousness which relieves the personages from the unnatural burden which, as single figures, they would have to sustain, make the group a charming and humane kind of conveyance ... in psychological terms ... it seems to offer the fascinations of an unexplained province in art.'[15]

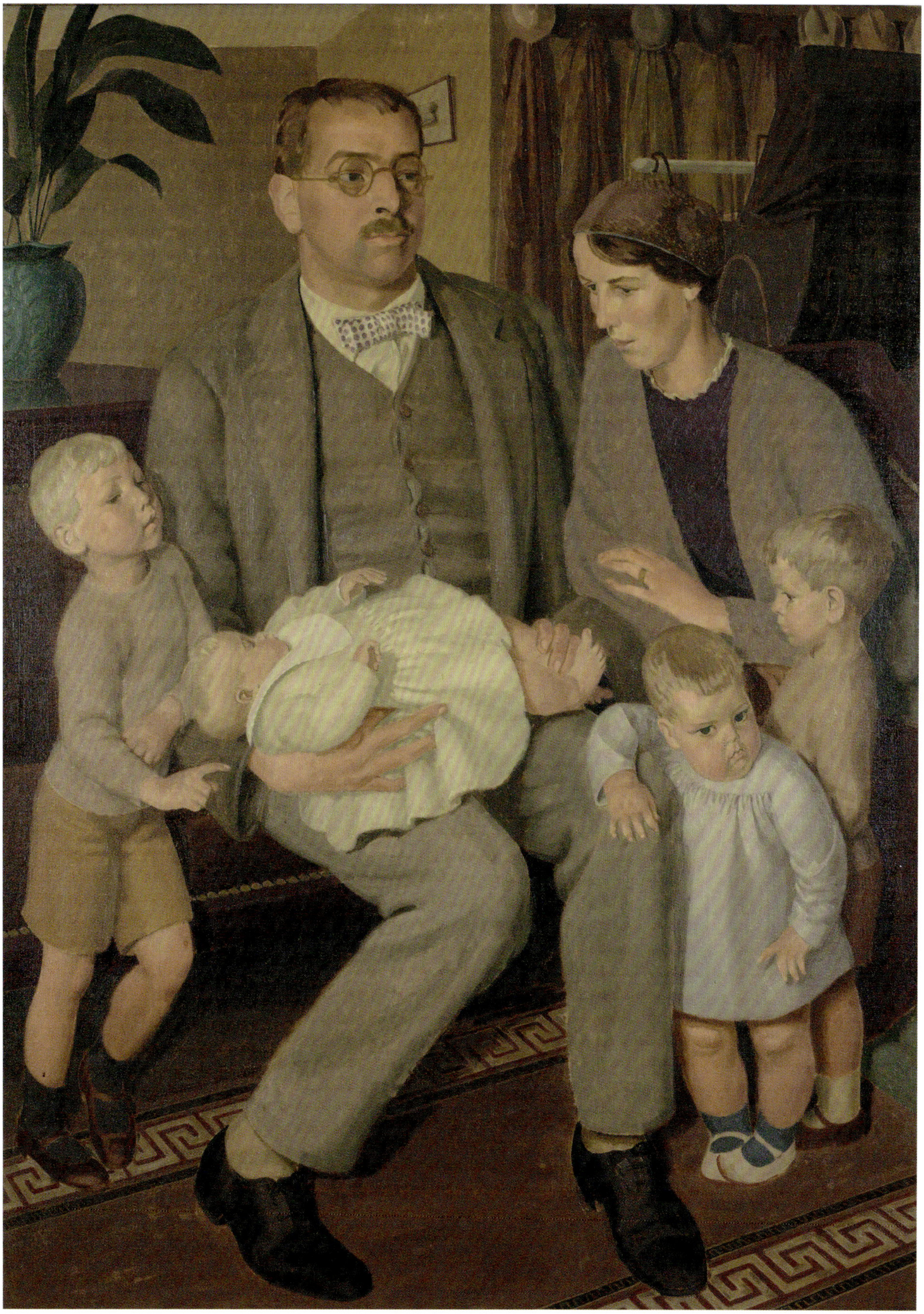

31

Romilly John, 1922

Oil on canvas, 51 × 40.9 cm
Manchester City Art Gallery

This portrait was formerly thought to depict the subject's brother David, but it was Romilly himself who confirmed his identity as the sitter shortly before the Manchester City Art Gallery Henry Lamb retrospective in 1984.[16] Lamb had acquired No. 10 Hill Street in Poole in February 1922, and the proximity to Dorelia at nearby Alderney Manor was unquestionably a significant factor in his choosing to make his home here. It was around this time that he executed this engaging and subtly sultry portrait, his sitter brimming with teenage attitude. Lamb had known most of Augustus John and Dorelia's children since they were born, also executing portraits of several of Augustus's children with his wife Ida, including David, Robin and Edwin. Romilly, who was sixteen when this portrait was painted, pursued a varied career, which took him from the R.A.F. to amateur physics via a stint in the Civil Service and a period working as a poet.

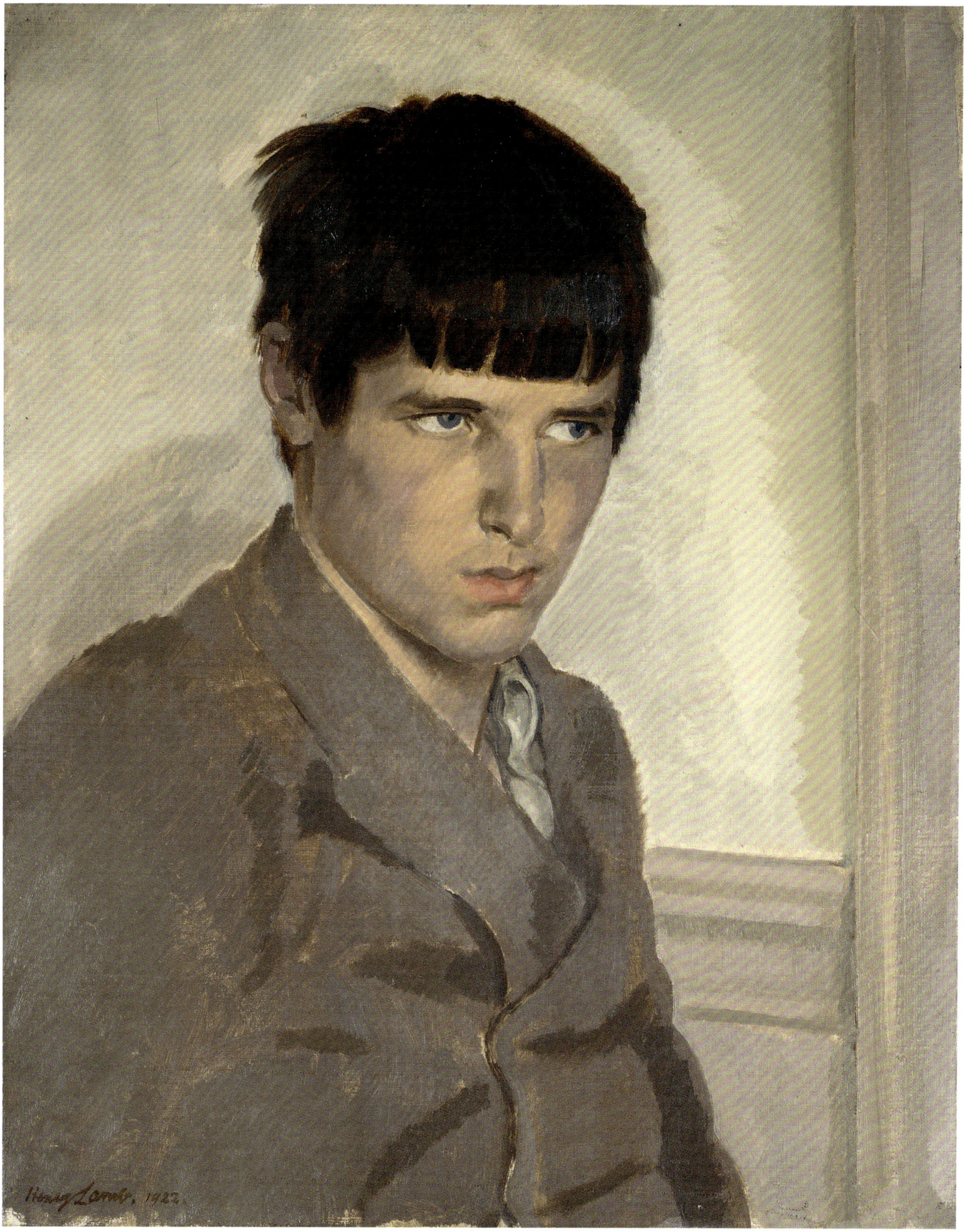
Henry Lamb, 1922.

32

Lord Moyne with his parents, 1930–36

Oil on canvas, 122 × 122 cm
The Hon. Daphne Guinness

Lamb's stylish portrait of Diana and Bryan Guinness was based on studies he had made while visiting the family's Irish retreat at Knockmaroon near Dublin. It had been over ten years since he painted *The Kennedy Family* (cat. 30) and the two group portraits show marked differences. The stylized formality of the Kennedy picture is in stark contrast to the suave elegance of the Guinness family, one of the most glamorous couples of the early 1930s, whom Lamb had come to know through his marriage to Pansy. Nevertheless, both portraits point to the artist's innate ability to construct an idiosyncratic and original composition from the kind of diverse elements that could have proved compromising in the hands of the wrong artist. Bryan Guinness later called this work 'a prophetic family group', a reference to the direction of the poses of the sitters, with Bryan fixing his gaze on the artist, his wife Diana facing away to the right of the painting. Diana was born Diana Mitford, one of the celebrated sisters. In 1936 she would leave Bryan to marry Sir Oswald Mosley. Bryan Guinness would later write a poem, 'The Composition', about this portrait, a poignant reflection on what was to come:

But, shaped in purple shadow overhead,
Incongruous, an Irish wolfhound looms,
Dark with foreboding, shaggy as a cloud,
He hangs his head in sad affection,
And guards the pattern of the composition.[17]

The most apparently stylized aspect of the composition is the wolfhound which hangs imposingly above the central group. The representation may not be quite as exaggerated as it first appears, however. John Fothergill mentioned Diana's wolfhound in his reminiscences as an innkeeper at Thame in Oxfordshire, commenting on its good nature and remarkable height of 3 ft 6 in.[18]

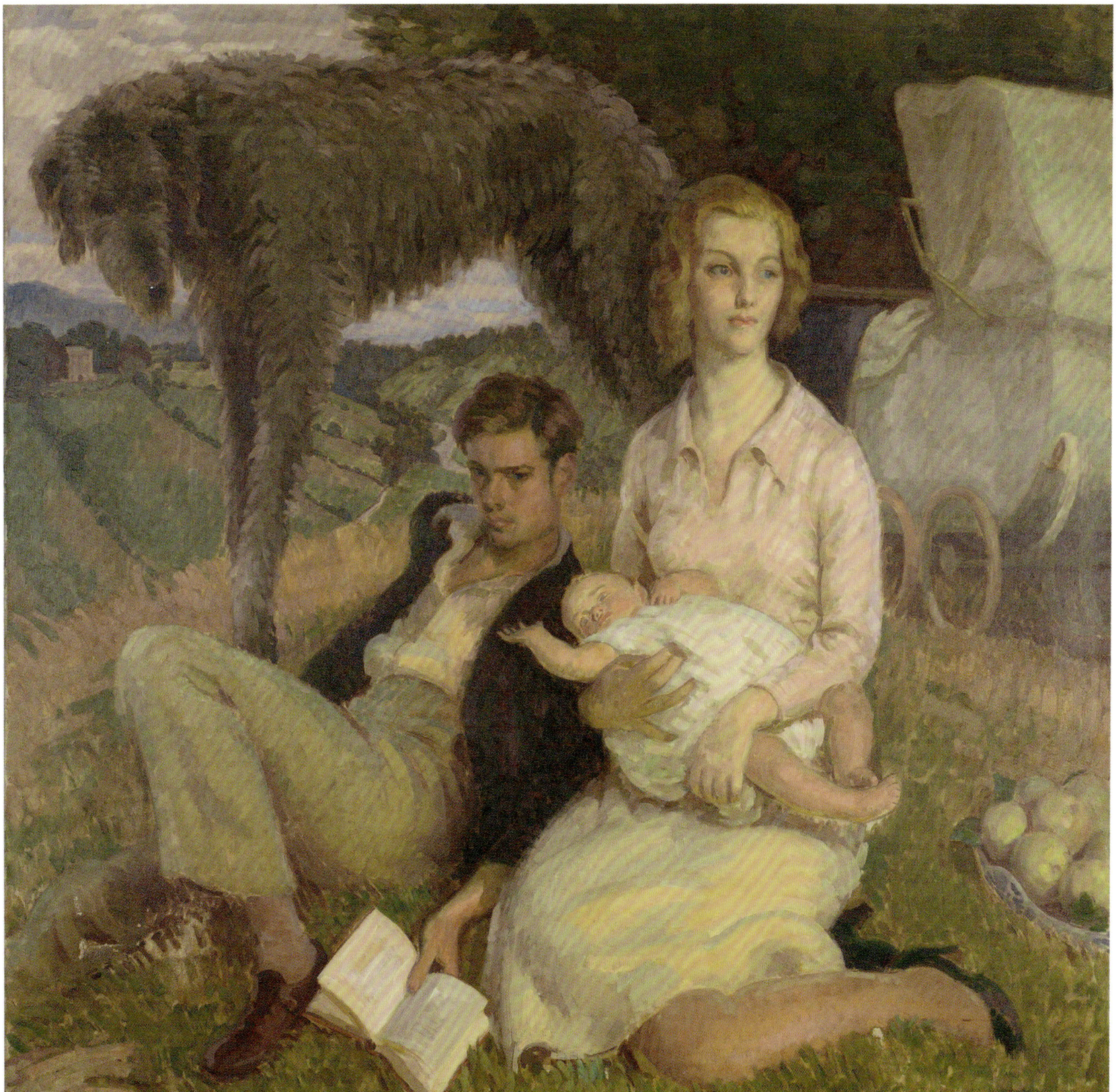

33

Evelyn Waugh, 1930

Oil on canvas, 74.6 × 62.3 cm
Private collection

Lamb met the novelist Evelyn Waugh while their respective fiancées (Lady Pansy Pakenham and Evelyn Gardner) were sharing furnished lodgings in Chelsea during the winter of 1927–28. The meeting became the catalyst for a now lost first portrait of Waugh, the sittings suggesting a meeting of minds, with Waugh evidently engaged by Lamb's intelligent conversation on art.[19] The portrait was reproduced in the *Studio* magazine that year and subsequently exhibited at the artist's one-man show at the Leicester Galleries in 1929, but otherwise appears to have occasioned little interest. A friend dismissively commented to Waugh, 'Lamb is having his show and there is a portrait of you, not one of his best things hanging on the walls of the Leicester Galleries. You look suspicious of everything in it.'[20]

As with two other of Lamb's most famous sitters, Lytton Strachey and Stanley Spencer, it would take a further attempt to capture fully the true essence of Waugh's personality. In the following year Waugh's marriage was on the verge of collapse. A letter from Lamb in August 1929 suggests a genuine concern for his new friend's predicament: 'I want you to count on my friendship & Pansy's too without a trace of partisan feeling .... Do please suggest yourself as a visitor if you feel inclined, it would be such a pleasure for us.'[21] Waugh was, indeed, to become a visitor to Coombe Bissett and in 1930 sat again for Lamb in what was to become the present work. The portrait must be the most iconic and memorable depiction of the writer. Its execution belies a suave sophistication not only reflecting the personality of the sitter but also the character of Lamb's best portraits from the 1930s. Holding the viewer with an uncompromisingly direct gaze, it presents Waugh as a figure of supreme confidence, belying any suggestion of the knocks that may have come his way from a recently failed marriage. Waugh and Lamb remained friends until the painter's death and corresponded occasionally during the late 1940s and early 1950s. In 1948 the idea of Waugh commissioning a replica of the portrait was proposed, but in the event this appears to have been abandoned.[22] Waugh and Pansy Lamb continued a long and intellectually charged correspondence until the writer's death in 1966.

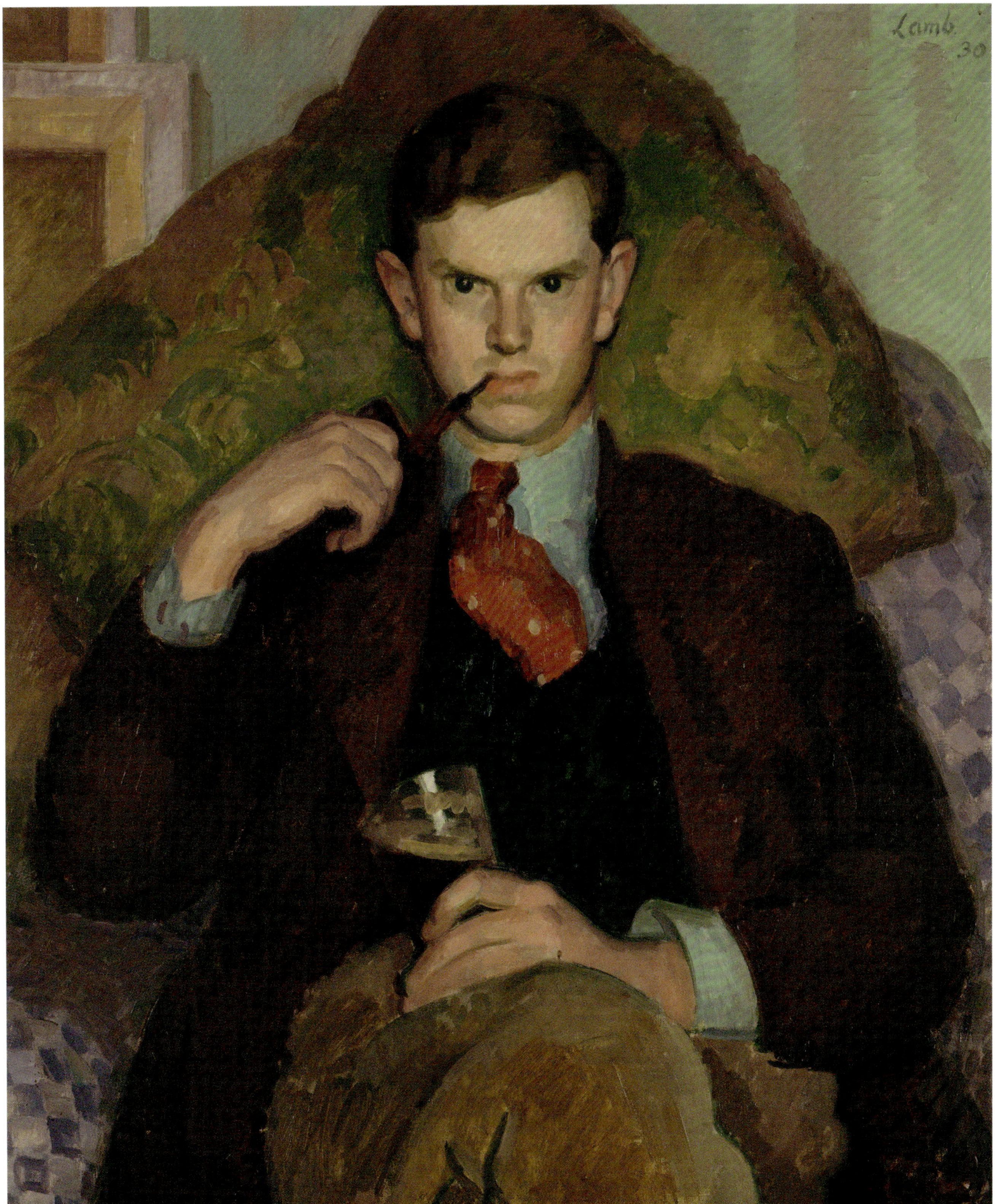
Lamb
30

34
Self-portrait, 1932

Oil on canvas, 73 × 63.5 cm
Private collection

Lamb's *Self-portrait* of 1932 is the artist's most significant attempt at the genre from the middle period of his career. By now he was firmly settled in Coombe Bissett, his first child Henrietta having been born in the previous year. This is something of a transitional work from a technical perspective, the handling of paint only beginning to hint at its subsequent breaking down into the *pointilliste* style of his later work. The early 1930s account for a number of Lamb's finest late portraits, amongst them *Evelyn Waugh* (cat. 33) and a fine portrait of Hon. Mrs Bryan Guinness (the future Diana Mosley) seated in her drawing room (1930, private collection). This picture certainly deserves its place alongside those works. The portrait also contains features that are common to all his self-portraits from the next three decades – each showing the now bespectacled painter staring with a piercing gaze, and at a slight angle, from the centre of the canvas. It is striking how similar in both pose and composition the present work is to his slightly later self-portrait of 1938 (private collection) – a head-and-shoulders portrait that almost resembles a snapshot of the 1932 portrait, the sitter only subtly aged in the intervening six years.[23]

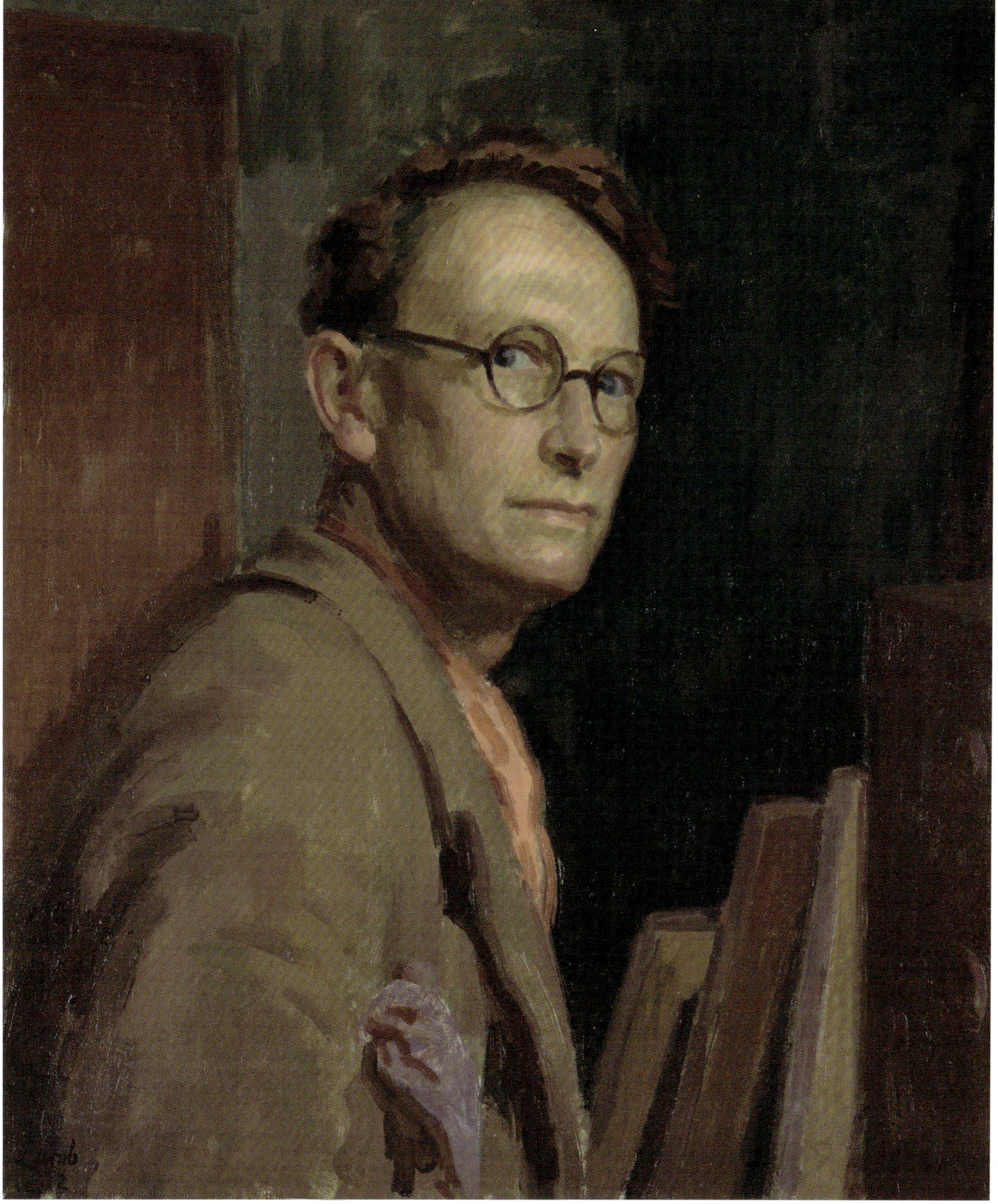

35

Sir Dan Godfrey, 1936

Oil on canvas, 135.5 × 85.5 cm
The Russell-Cotes Art Gallery & Museum, Bournemouth

As a great meeting of Lamb's dual passions for music and art, this monumental portrait of the distinguished Bournemouth conductor Sir Dan Godfrey should have been the commission that gave Lamb more pleasure than any other. In the event it was to attract an unfortunate level of local controversy and something of a personality clash between artist and conductor.

The Bournemouth Symphony Orchestra had been founded as the Bournemouth Municipal Orchestra by Godfrey in 1893. Initially comprising a group of wind players and a drummer, the ensemble's flexibility was designed to allow the possibility of open-air concerts on Bournemouth pier. Soon evolving into a full orchestra, it went on to champion the work of British composers in particular, including Edward Elgar and Gustav Holst. Godfrey is still to this day the orchestra's longest serving principal conductor. Lamb had followed the orchestra closely for over a decade before this work was painted, its concerts in the 1920s providing a valuable refuge during his many lonely moments living in nearby Poole. He had made early attempts to paint its musicians, executing a wash study and small oil of the orchestra in the full throes of performance, but seemed displeased with the results. When exhibited at the Royal Academy in 1937, the portrait of Sir Dan Godfrey garnered widespread praise, *The Stage* declaring: 'His picture is a tour de force of the exhibition and a highly finished one at that'.[24] This reception masks a more mixed reaction when the portrait was unveiled in Bournemouth, however. The work had been paid for through a subscription scheme by British composers as a tribute to Sir Dan, and was unveiled following a concert at the Bournemouth Pavilion in March 1936. Despite a polite reception on its unveiling Sir Dan was said to have detested the picture on first sight.[25] Even more damning criticism was to come from the then curator of the Russell-Cotes Museum in Bournemouth, N. L. Silvester: 'I do not like it and no one whom I have met has liked it .... Artists should realise their limitations .... They should understand that sitters wish to be portrayed as ordinary people see them.'[26] The picture even occasioned a cartoon in *Punch,* 'Muscular Development of the neck induced by the continual acknowledgement of applause',[27] a reference to the awkwardness of the turning pose that many perceived in the picture. Despite this controversy, Lamb's portrait is certainly one of his most ambitious and has a satisfyingly graphic quality that is not wholly unsuccessful. Music was clearly much on the artist's mind as he enjoyed family life in the late 1930s. Some six years later he would exhibit his celebrated family portrait *The Artist's Family*, in which he is seated at a piano, one of the few direct references in his work to his own not inconsiderable talents as an amateur classical musician.

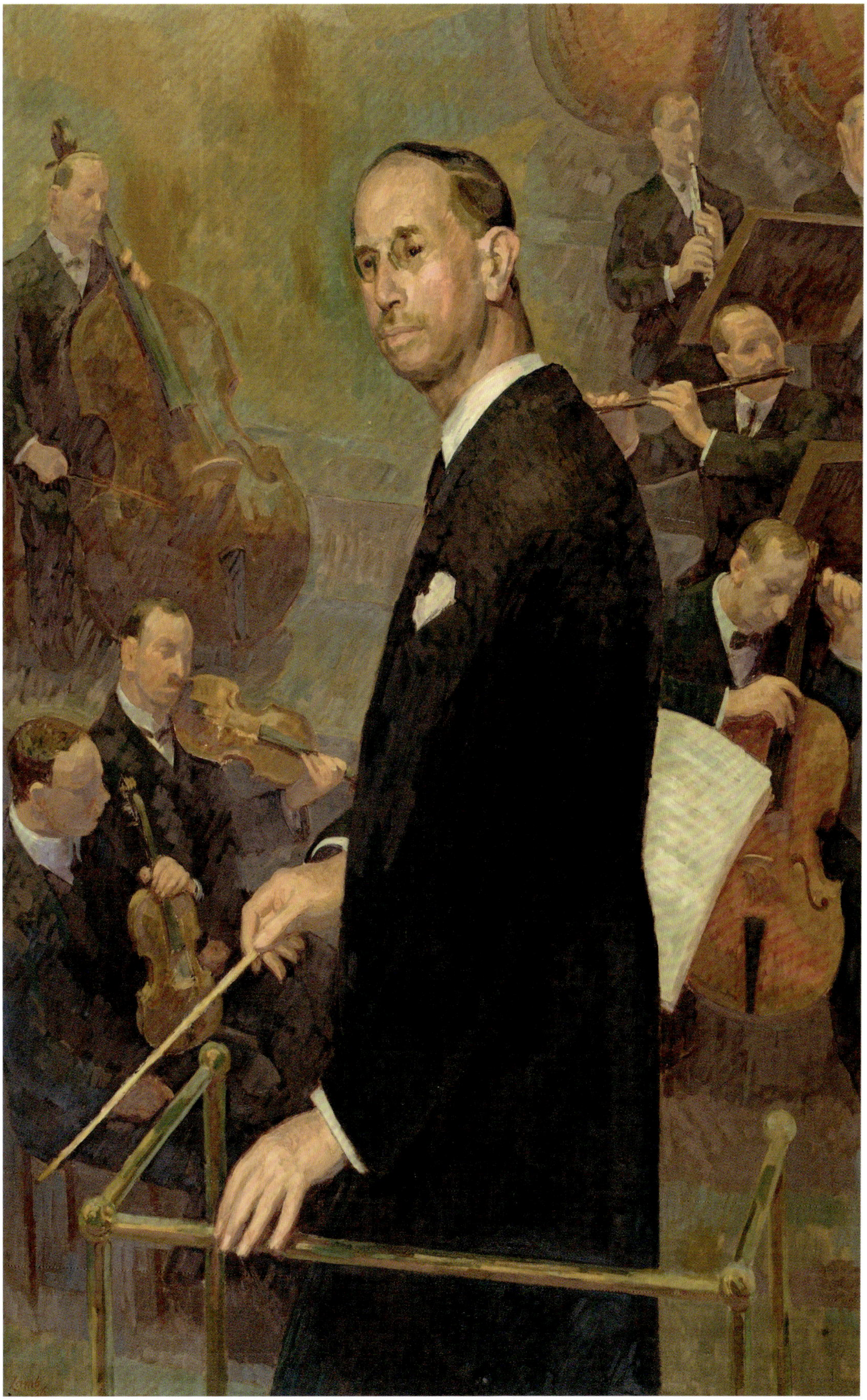

36

Little still life with a pansy, 1928

Oil on panel, 20.3 × 26.7 cm
The Henry Lamb Estate

Still-life painting did not feature as a major part of Lamb's output, and he never submitted a still life to a public exhibition at either the New English Art Club or the Royal Academy. There is, nevertheless, some evidence that he enjoyed commercial success with them, and they appear regularly in his commercial shows (the present work was exhibited at his second one-man show at the Leicester Galleries, in 1929). Such works reveal him to be a talented still-life painter, allowing him to explore stronger and more diverse pigments within his palette range than his more subdued work in landscape and portraiture allowed. The present work is a particularly successful example, executed in an almost Whistlerian, tonal style that recalls similar work by Sir William Nicholson at around the same date. His choice of flower here is perhaps not coincidental; he would marry Pansy in the same year.

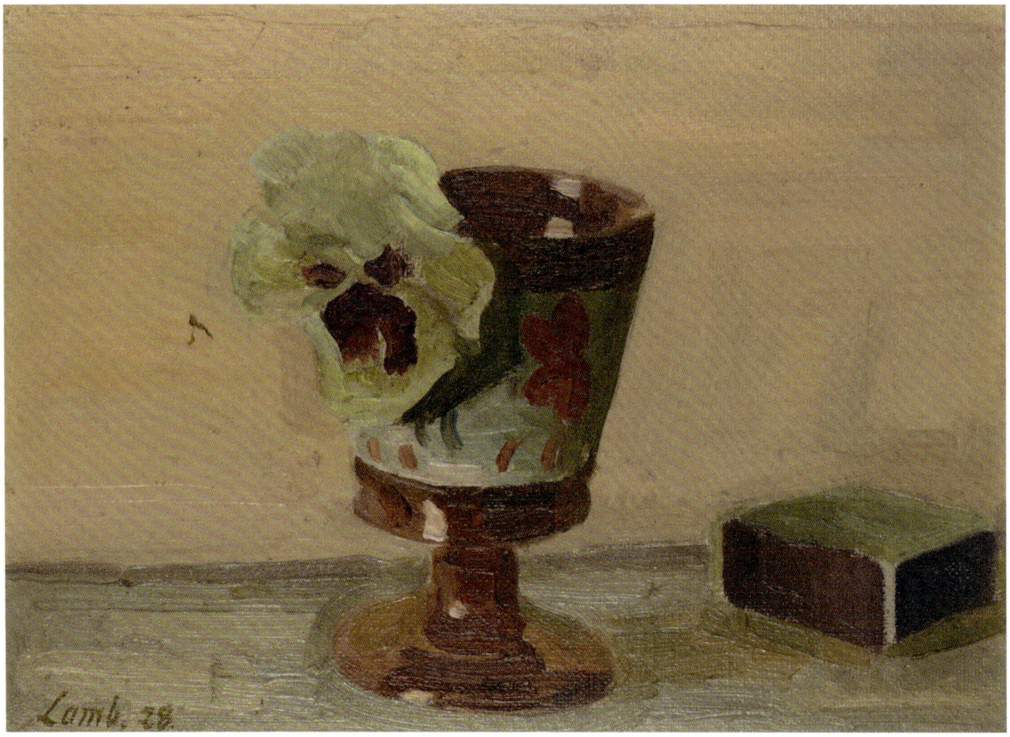

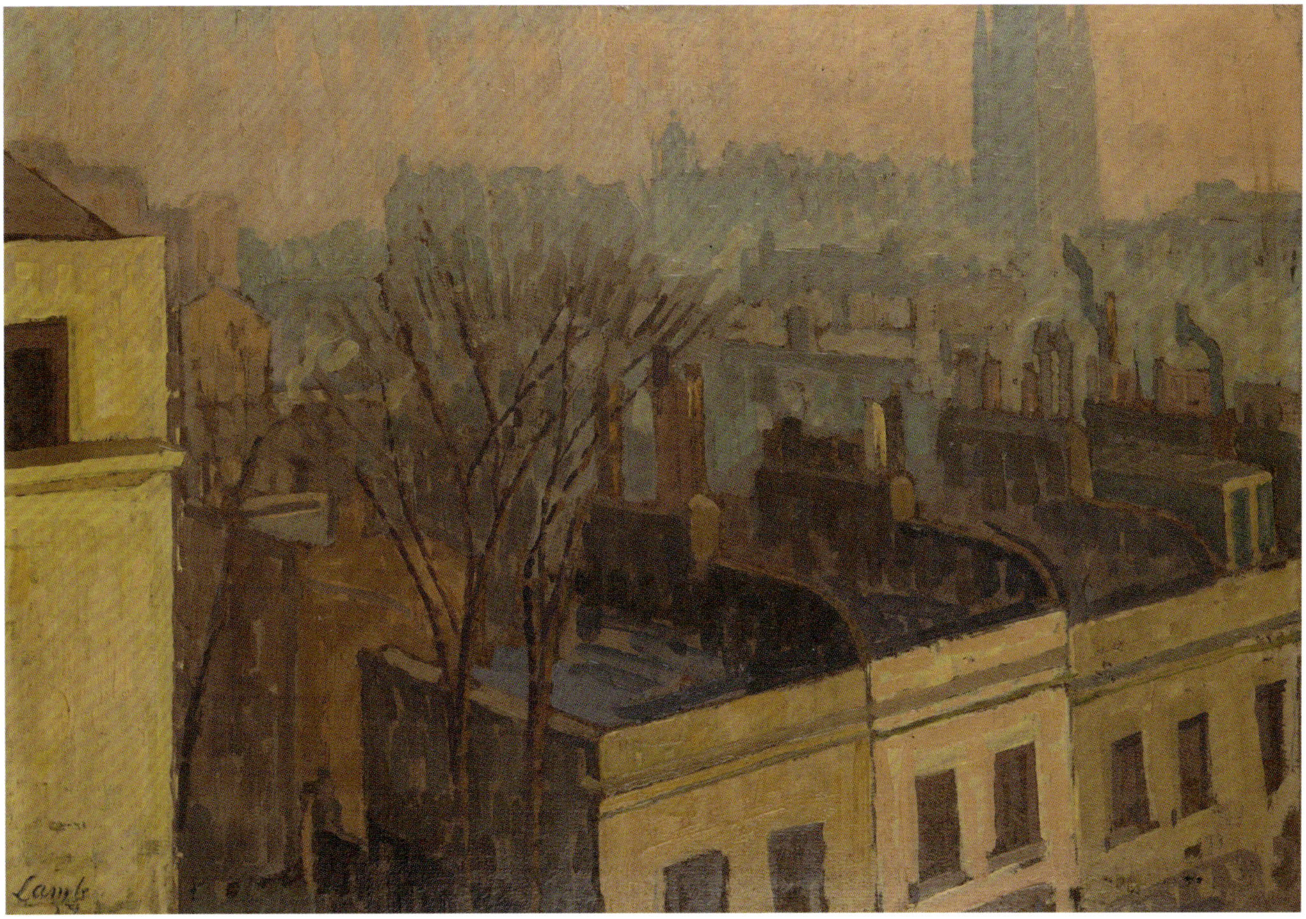

37

Kensington Roofs, 1927

Oil on board, 44.5 × 59.5 cm
The Henry Lamb Estate

Lamb relinquished his studio at the Vale Hotel on Hampstead Heath in 1926, and in November rented another just north of Kensington High Street at No. 20 Gordon Place. This view was painted there, the winter sunset colours and bare trees suggesting a date early in 1927. In April that year it was exhibited at Lamb's first one-man show at the Leicester Galleries.[1] Lamb attempts here to emulate the highly successful rooftop views made from his Hill Street home in Poole. He successfully conveys the greater expanse of the larger city, and the result is in marked contrast to the claustrophobic impressions of Poole's small lanes. In both subject and execution it is one of only a few works that show elements of Camden Town influence, particularly the work of Malcolm Drummond, whose cityscapes likewise focus on the abstract form of the streets and buildings rather than precise rendering of detail. Sadly, Lamb rarely attempted such views after the 1920s. This work was later acquired by Pansy Lamb, which is particularly understandable given that her relationship with Henry, and the lease on Gordon Place, began around the time this was painted.

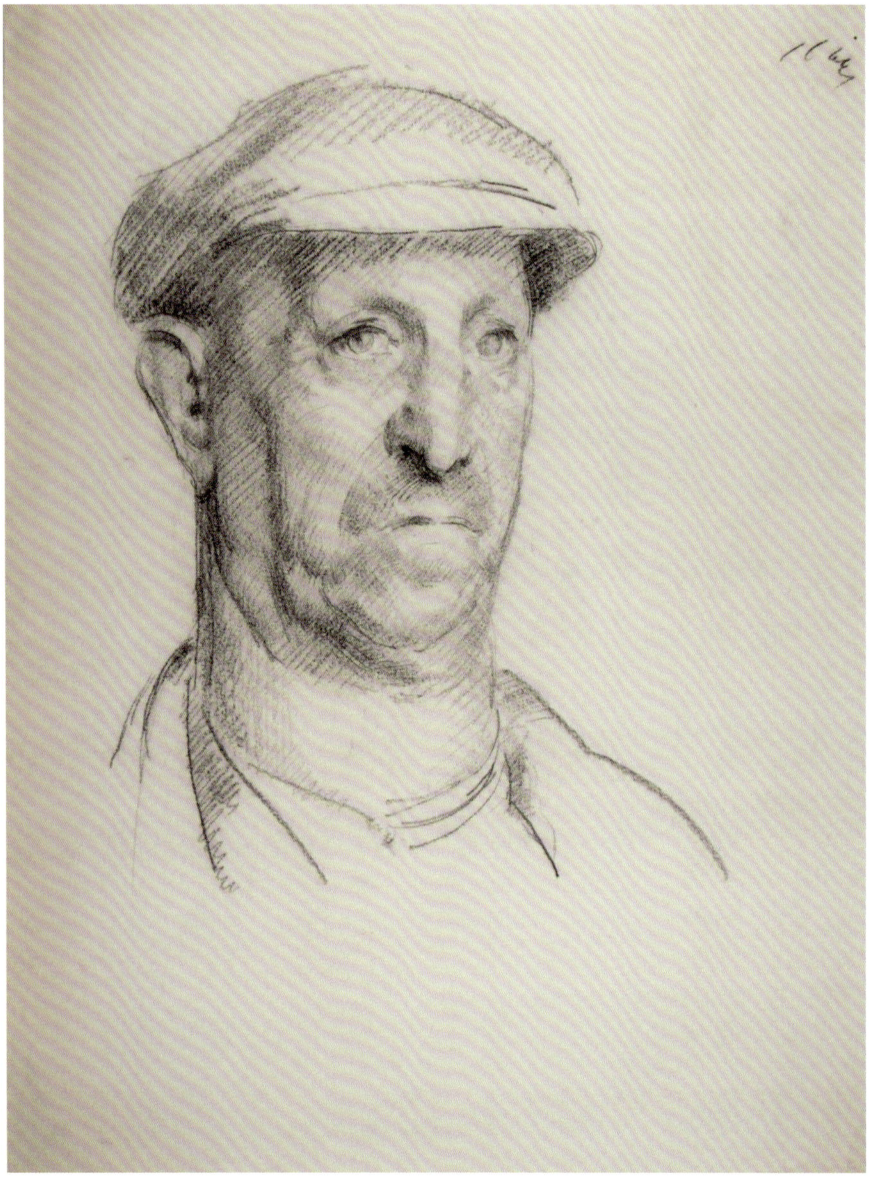

38

Mr Harris, Coombe Bissett Gardener, 1930s

Pencil on paper, 380 × 280 mm
The Henry Lamb Estate

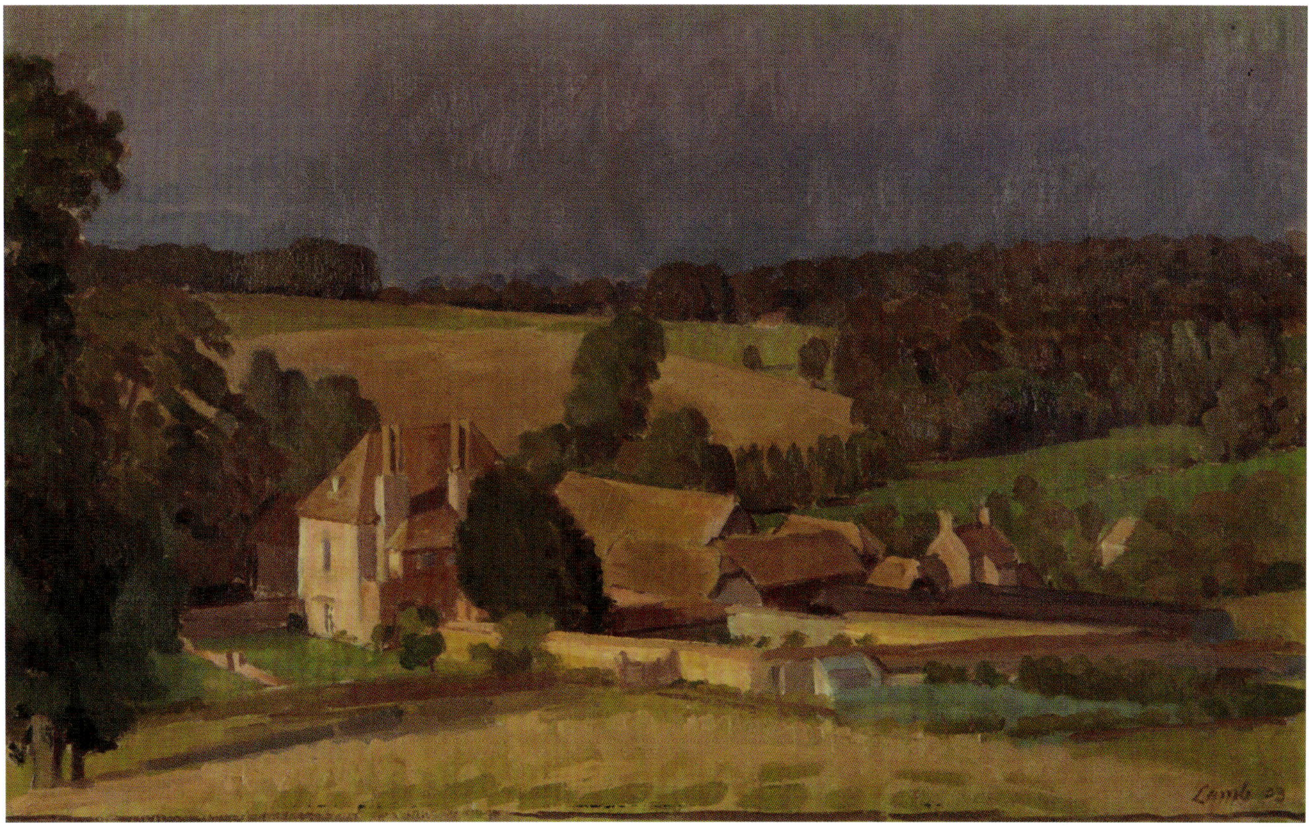

39

Odstock Manor, 1933

Oil on panel, 47 × 68 cm
Private collection

The Lambs benefited from the company of a number of like-minded and influential neighbours following their move to Coombe Bissett. Amongst them was Hugo Pitman, who lived at Odstock Manor and who probably met Lamb through the Contemporary Art Society, where Pitman served on the executive committee. Pitman had a fine collection of contemporary British art of the period and owned a number of works by Augustus John, including one of the artist's most significant works, *Lyric Fantasy*. This attractive landscape shows Odstock Manor nestled in its picturesque setting in the Chalke Valley. Intriguingly, the work appears to be something of a spontaneous landscape study and Lamb did not identify Odstock Manor directly as a subject, simply titling the work on its reverse *House in the Chalke Valley, Salisbury*.

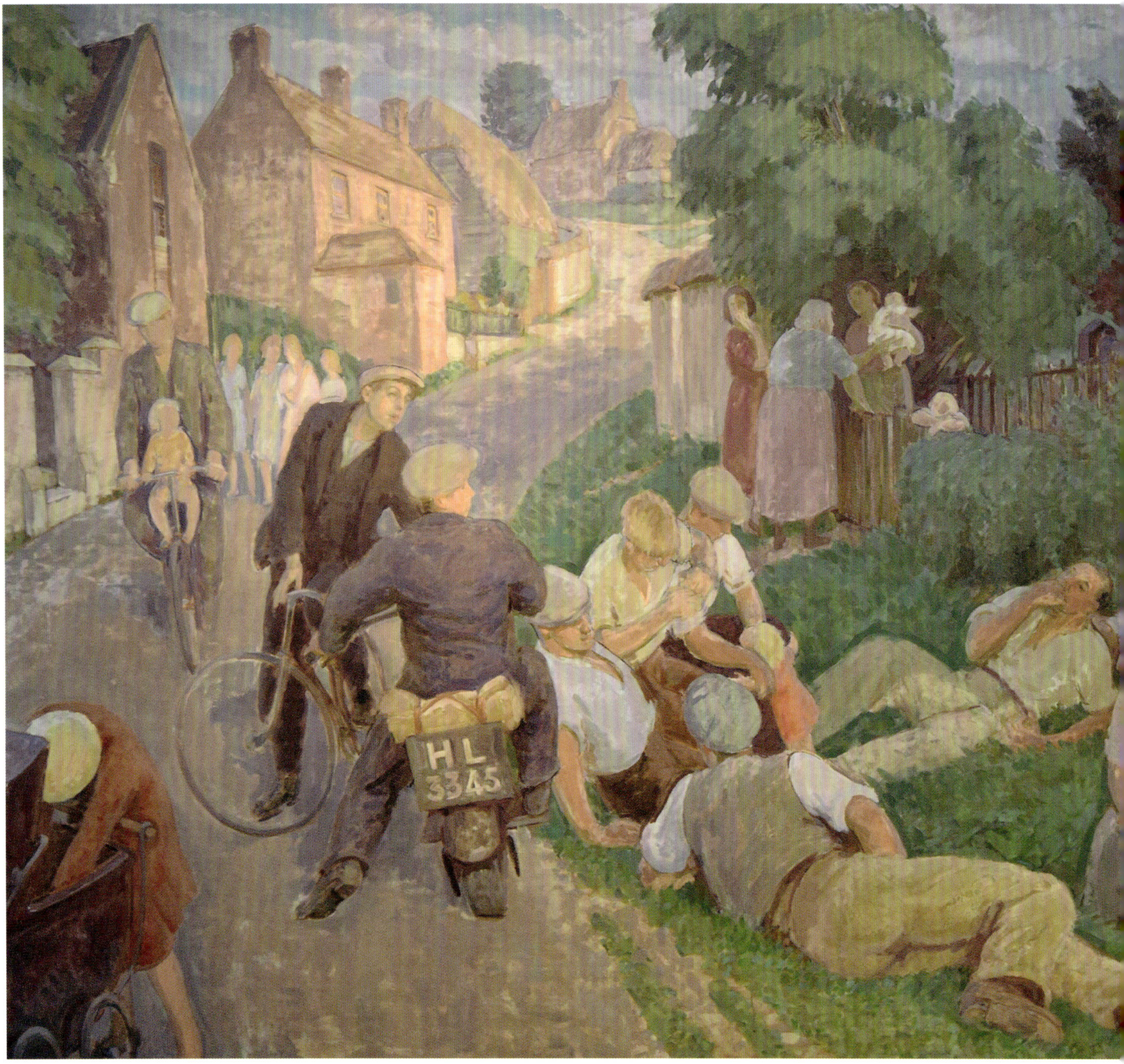
HL
3345

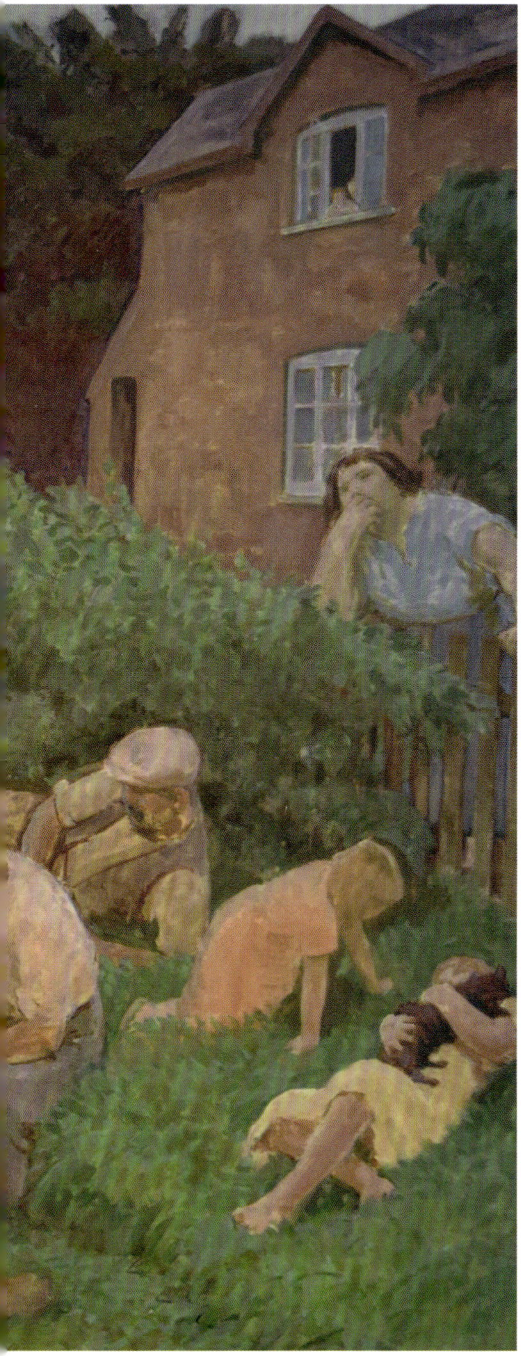

40

Evening at the Village, 1935

Oil on canvas, 163 × 261 cm
The Henry Lamb Estate

Lamb's bustling conversation piece *Evening in the Village* is a joyous celebration of the village of Coombe Bissett, which by the date of the painting had been his family home for some seven years. Constructed around the shape of the village's distinctive winding road, the scene possesses Lamb's characteristic quality of falling between the idealized and the earthily realistic. Genre paintings that capture a sense of place are central to Lamb's work, and the roots for the present piece can be traced right back to *Fisherfolk* in 1913. There too, his careful synthesis of figure and landscape served to encapsulate his view of the Irish island. A closer compositional comparison can be found in Lamb's busy Poole work *Football Edition* (1926, location unknown), at the centre of which a group of boys are perched eagerly on their bicycles, echoed here by the motorcyclists. As always in his more sophisticated compositions, the artist worked on the painting through numerous compositional studies, amongst these a watercolour of the motorcyclists (which he also made into a Christmas card),[2] an oil sketch based on the figures to the right of the picture and a number of sketchbook studies.[3] It is notable how Lamb was moving away from Stanley Spencer's more exaggerated brand of stylization by the 1930s, although an interesting (if perhaps coincidental) comparison has been made between the right side of the painting and a work by Spencer from the same year, *By the River*.[4] Lamb's style is perhaps more illustrative here, conjuring up the spirit of his scene rather than attempting more studied portrait-making of its many figures. It strongly anticipates the style of painting that Lamb would use to good effect in the military genre subjects he would execute as an official war artist over five years later. One visitor to Coombe Bissett at this date was the future poet laureate John Betjeman, who wrote the following verse perhaps as a reaction to the present work (or conceivably vice versa):

Oh, the calm of Coombe Bissett is tranquil and deep
Where Ebble flows soft in her downland asleep
And the beauty to me came pushing a pram
In the shape of the sweet Pansy, Felicia, Lamb.[5]

41

Pansy with her two daughters, c.1934

Oil on board, 48 × 33 cm
The Henry Lamb Estate

This charming and swiftly executed oil sketch of Pansy with the couple's two daughters Henrietta and Felicia possesses a strongly graphic quality which almost recalls a pen and ink drawing. Although the picture is undated, Felicia is evidently less than a year old, suggesting a date for the work of around 1934. It is strongly reminiscent of Augustus John's many sketches of Dorelia with her children from some 25 years earlier. The painting's style of execution is rarely seen elsewhere in Lamb's work, however, suggesting a degree of experimentation at this date that would ultimately give way to the more painterly technique of his later portraits and genre works.

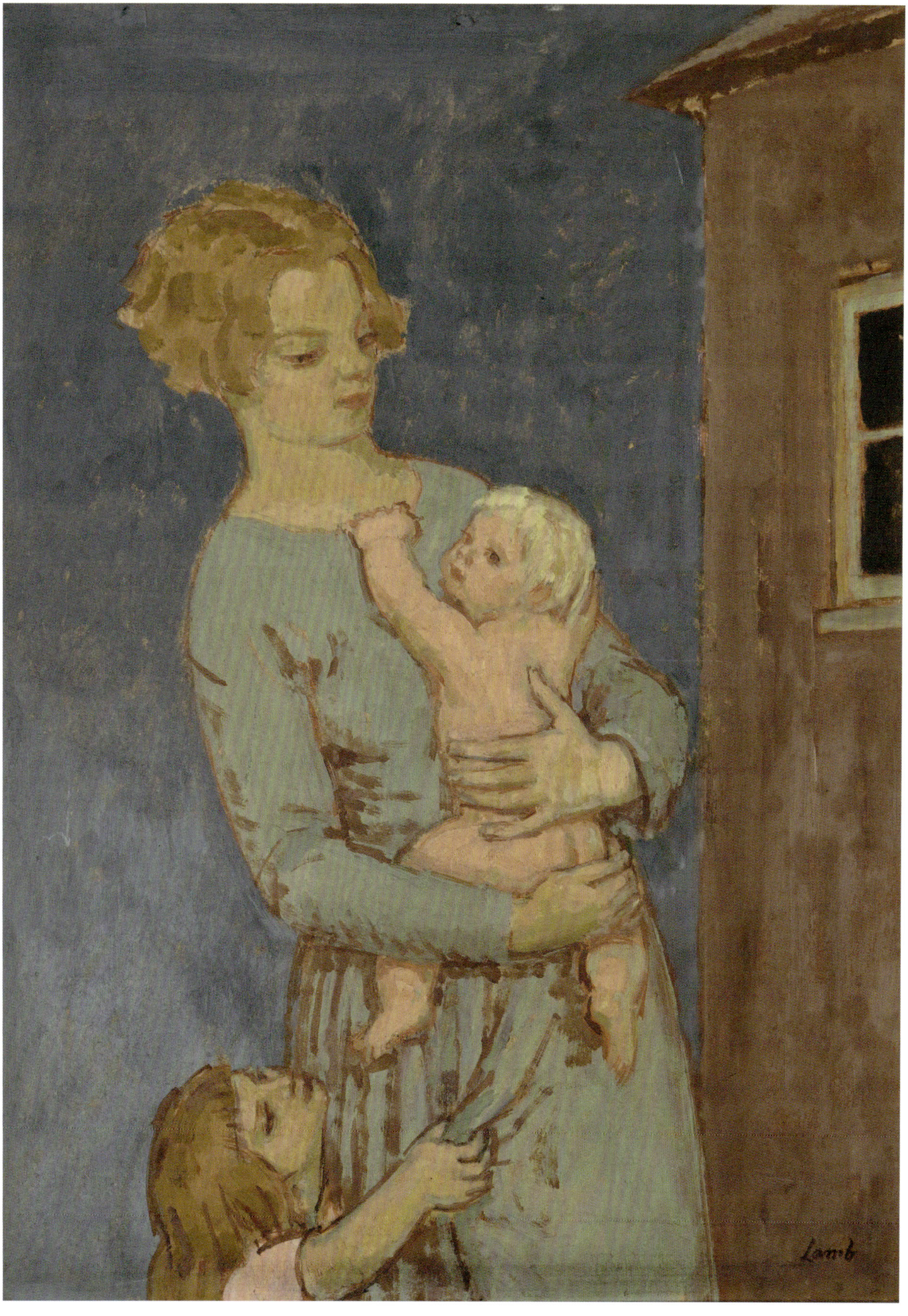
Lamb

42

The Infant, 1933

Oil on canvas, 125 × 107 cm
The Henry Lamb Estate

Following his marriage to Pansy in August 1928, Lamb proved astonishingly swift in his embrace of domestic life. In the same year he acquired their family home, 'Brookside', in Coombe Bissett near Salisbury, and in the next decade the couple's three children were born – Henrietta (1931), Felicia (1933) and Valentine (1939). *The Infant* is one of the artist's finest evocations of family life and was exhibited in the celebrated showcase exhibition in Pittsburgh at the Carnegie Institute, where he had had some success with earlier work, in particular *Death of a Peasant*, which had been shown there as part of an historical survey of British art a few years earlier in 1925. The date of 1933 suggests that the work probably depicts Pansy with their second child Felicia, who was born that year. The work, with its luminous warm palette, is strikingly sensitive, no more so than in the loving downward gaze Pansy casts over her new child. From here onwards his family and children became central to both his working and non-working life, Pansy's cousin and Lamb's close friend the novelist Anthony Powell writing: '... he behaved as if no one else had ever produced children – at least none like his own – confounding all who had shaken ... heads about his reactions to domesticity'.[6]

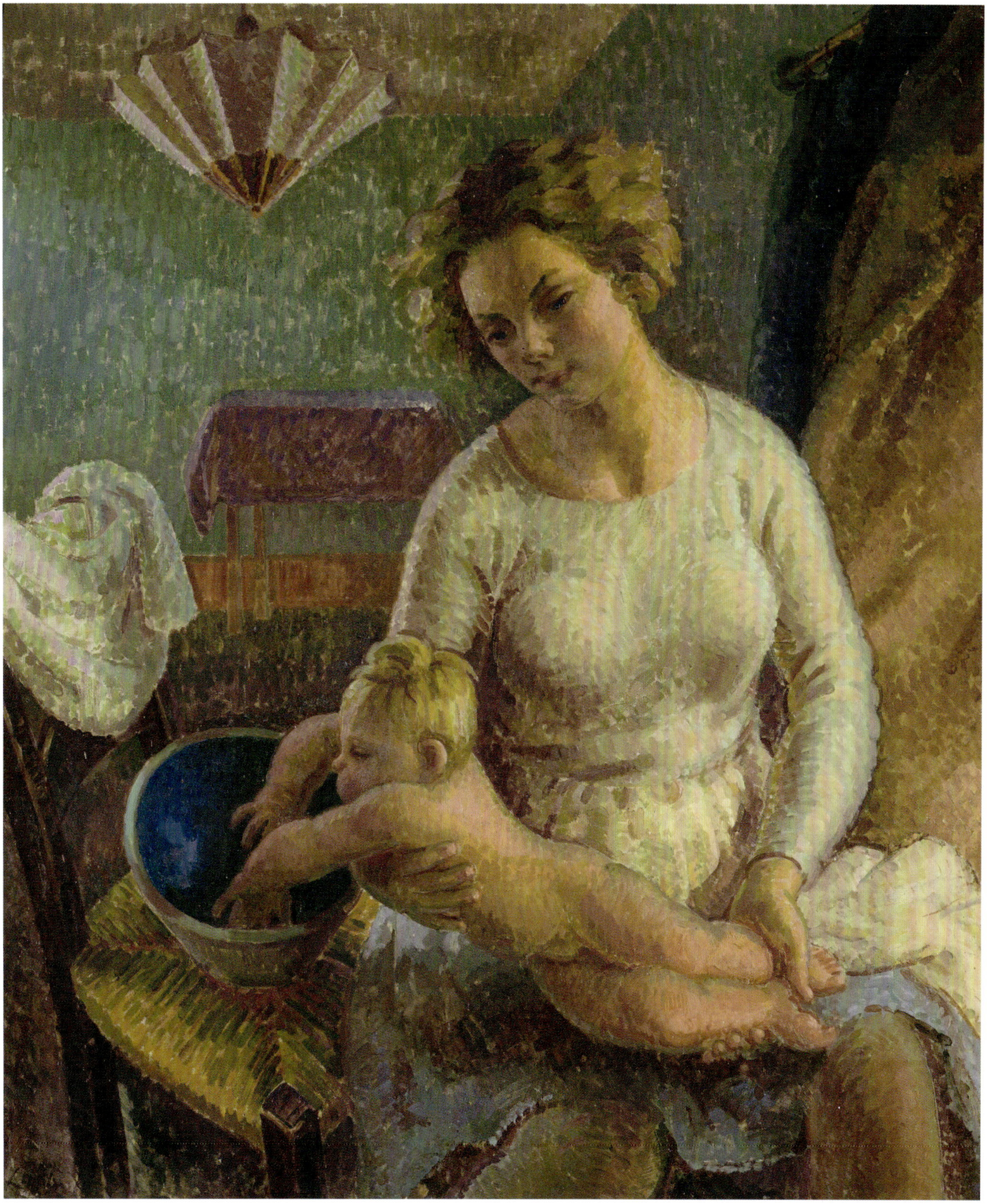

43

The Artist's Daughters with Nelson, 1939–40

Oil on canvas, 155 × 124.5 cm
The Henry Lamb Estate

The artist's youngest daughter Felicia remembers the cat in the present work. It was called Nelson (having been born on Trafalgar Day), and was quite unable to pose successfully for this monumental painting. The cat was added later from studies, and she recalls (as with other family group portraits) sitting for the portrait separately from her sister Henrietta. The resulting painting is a deliberately old fashioned, almost pastiche-classical work. It shows some strong similarities with the work of Thomas Gainsborough, of whom (particularly in his letters whilst a Tate trustee) Lamb appears to have been an admirer. The work bears some interesting comparison with paintings like the double portrait of the *Villebois Boys* from c.1783 or Gainsborough's own touching depiction of his two daughters holding a butterfly of c.1756.

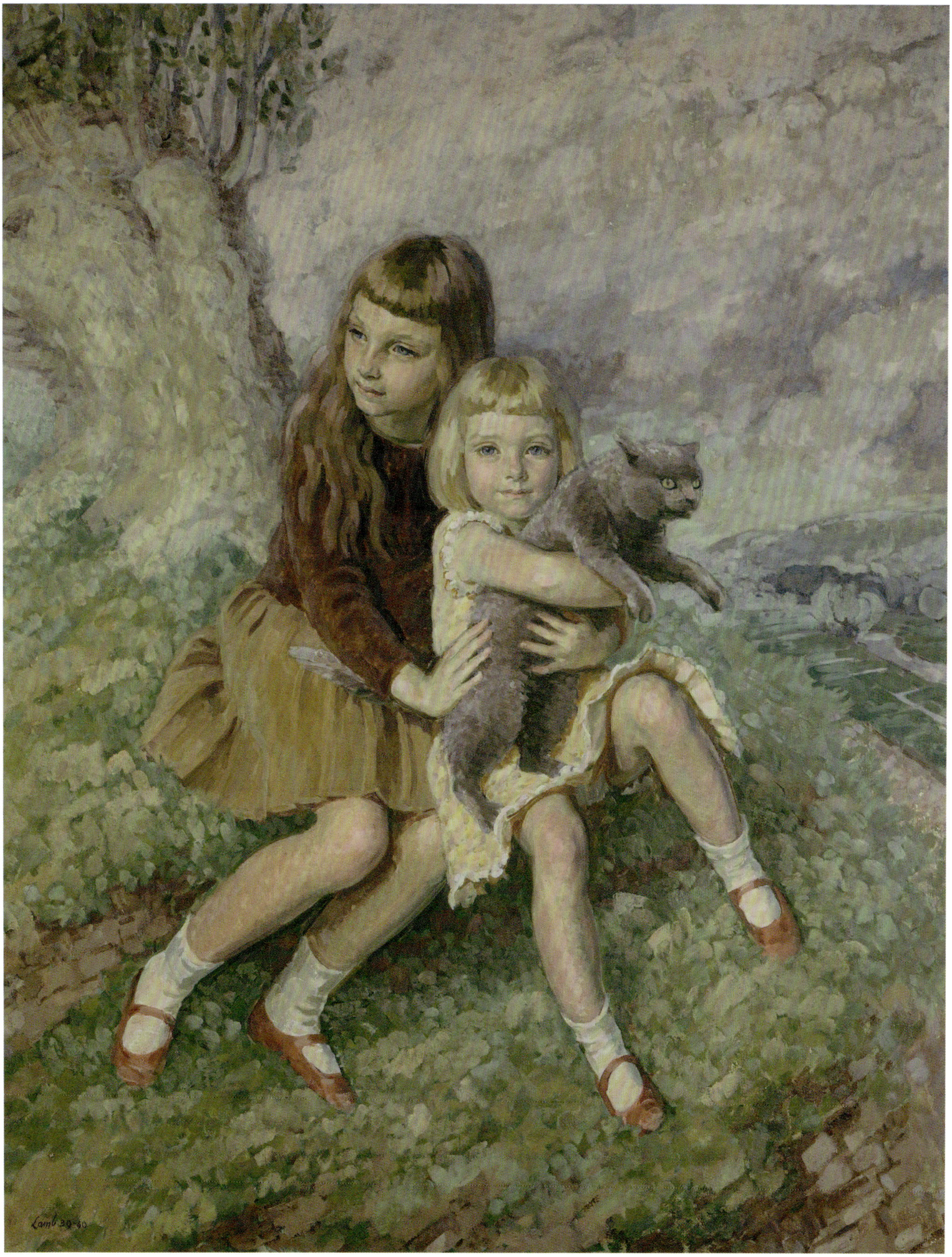
Lamb 39-40

44

Study for *The Artist's Family*, c.1943

Oil on canvas, 51 × 41 cm
Private collection

The ambitious group portrait *The Artist's Family* (Tate) can be seen as the culmination of a significant body of domestic subjects that were begun of his wife Pansy soon after their move to Coombe Bissett in 1928. These themes were then developed through numerous paintings of his children throughout the 1930s. Although many portrait studies exist of the children individually, in groups or with Pansy, this the only work (with its studies) that depicts the entire family. Its complex and intricate composition came about through a series of smaller studies and portraits that appear both as smaller paintings and as countless designs in the artist's sketchbooks. At its heart is a development of the mother and child theme – a motif that is treated in much the same way here as it had been in his sketches of Pansy with the two elder children from the first half of the 1930s. The sketchbook drawings suggest that Lamb struggled with what was to be a complex composition, particularly as to how Felicia (seated on the central chair) engaged with her mother and younger brother and Lamb himself, who at one point is depicted to the left-hand side of the composition looking in towards the rest of his family on the right. Keith Clements has observed that the long gestation of the work (begun in 1940 but not finished until 1943) accounts for the slightly disjointed composition. He also rightly describes it as upbeat, 'like a celebration of his being home again'.[7] It is also a work, however, that strangely highlights the painter's isolation. Like *The Tea Party* some fifteen years earlier, Lamb is cast adrift to one side of the composition, with his back to us and facing in towards his clavichord. Despite its deficiencies the painting was sufficiently highly regarded to be acquired by the Chantry Bequest and presented to the Tate Gallery in 1961, a year after Lamb's death. The present work is the most complete oil sketch for the painting and arguably contains a freshness and spontaneity that the final painting lacks.

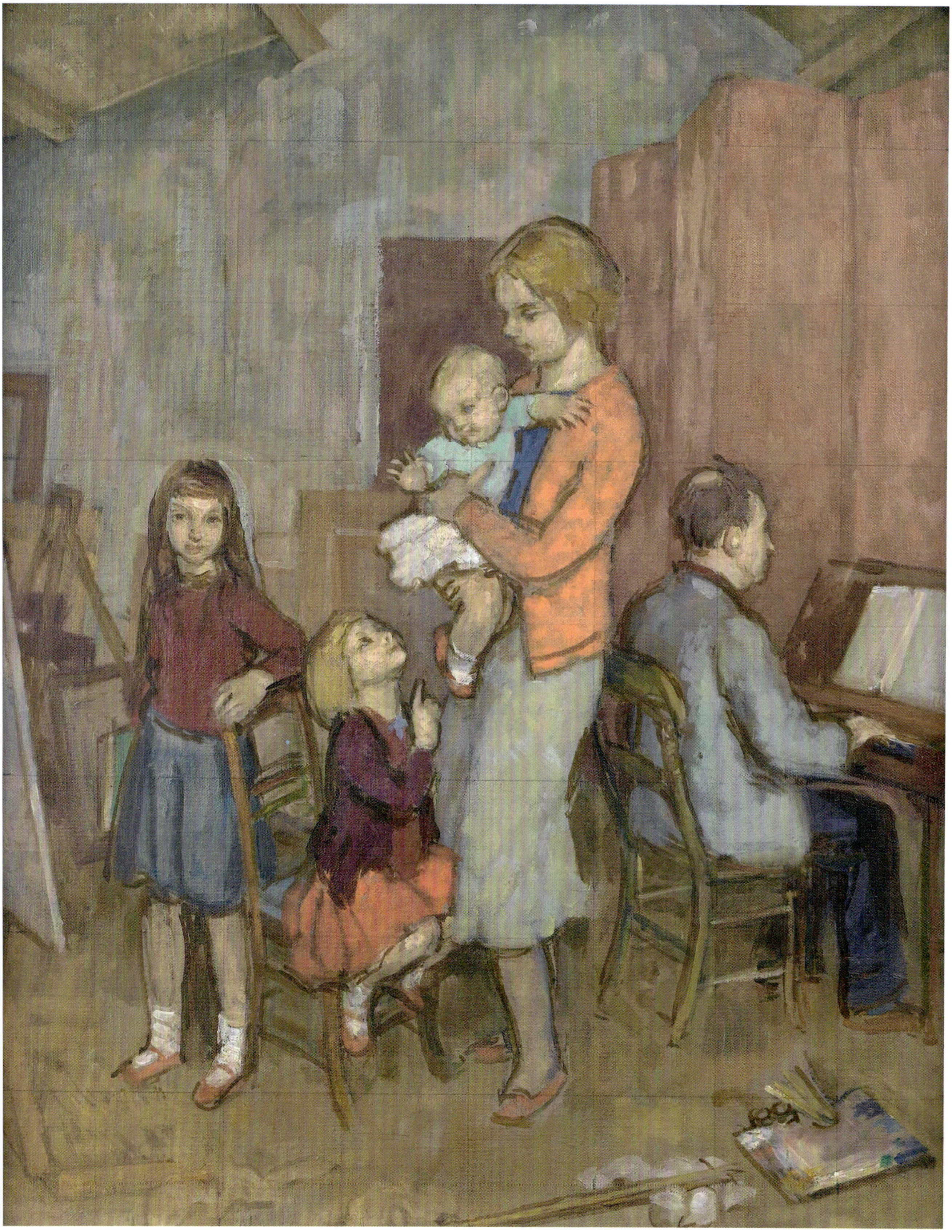

45

Henrietta, Felicia and Valentine Reading

Oil on canvas, 62 × 98 cm
The Henry Lamb Estate

This ambitious group portrait, probably begun in the late 1940s, is evidence of the success that Lamb achieved through making detailed portraits of each of his children in separate sittings. Here he pieces together the seemingly disjointed individual portrait studies into a pleasingly contrived final painting. It is an unusually sophisticated and modern example of his work in this genre, the strikingly empty red background highlighting the rather abstract form created in the grouping of the three children. The apparent age of Valentine in this painting does not fit with that of his sisters, both of whom were several years older than him. This might suggest that the work was composed at a much later date using studies of his children from earlier stages in their lives.

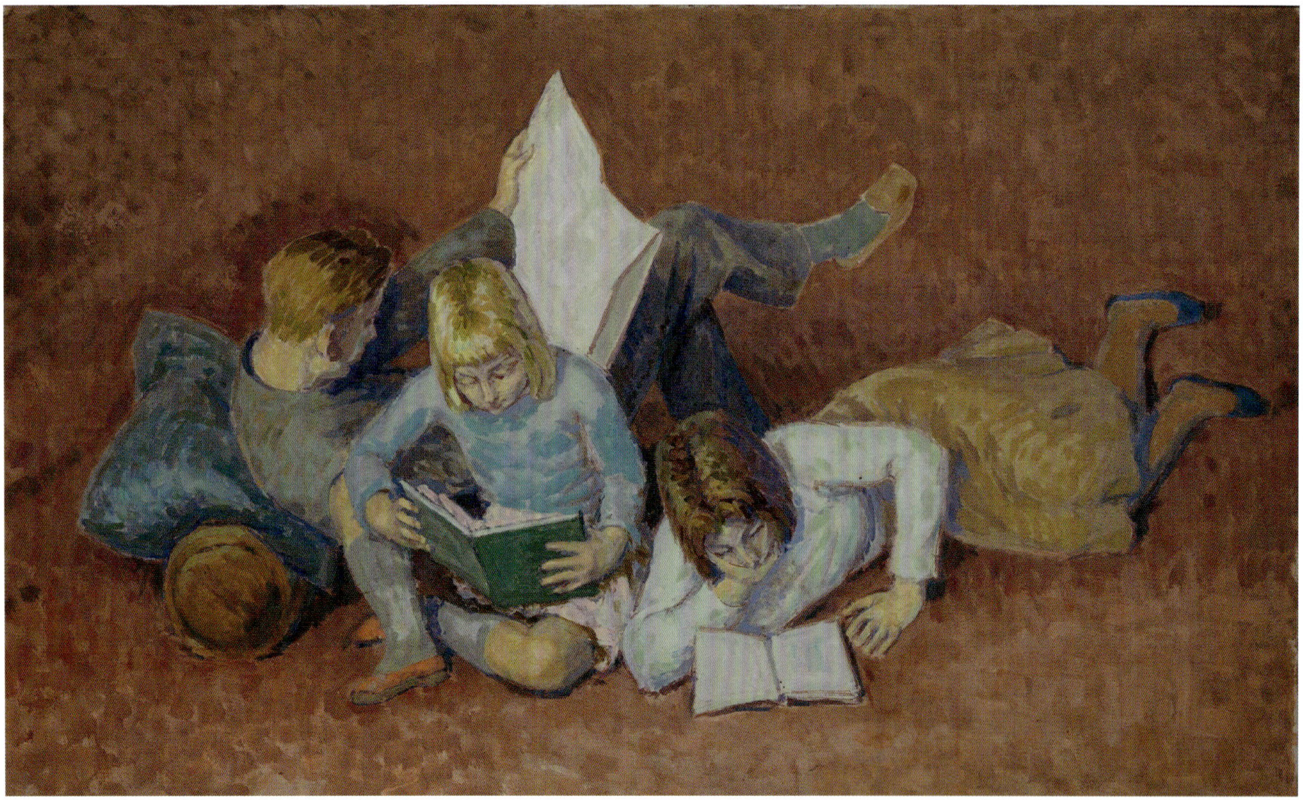

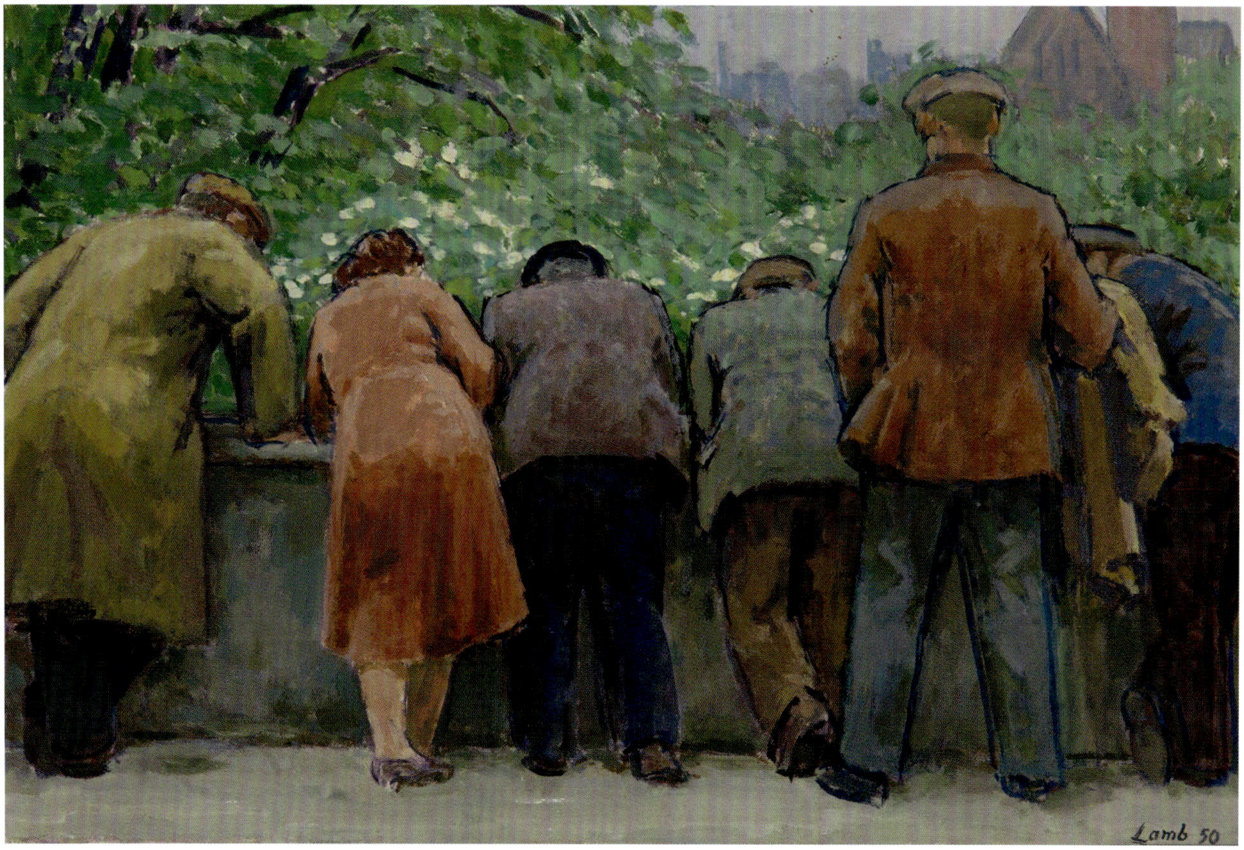

46

Aberdeen, 1950

Oil on panel, 45 × 59.5 cm
Private collection

Humorous scenes depicting groups of people observed unknowingly and frequently from behind are a regular motif in some of Lamb's later subject paintings. A similar composition (effectively reversed – with his subjects facing forward) can be seen in *Over the Garden Wall*, which was presented by the Contemporary Art Society for Wales to the Cyfartha Castle Museum and Gallery in 1947. Both works reflect something of the playful and witty influence of Edward Ardizzone, the illustrator and fellow war artist from the Second World War. The location of the present work has been identified as Union Terrace Gardens in Aberdeen behind a well-known statue of Robert Burns. The then prestigious Caledonian Hotel was situated directly opposite. It has been suggested that the crowd is looking down on a game of outdoor draughts being played (as was customary) on a lower level.[8] Lamb was one of a number of academicians who visited Aberdeen, probably as an assessor at Gray's School of Art. The painting was exhibited at Lamb's third and final one-man show at the Leicester Galleries in December 1956 (no. 12).

47

Henrietta with Flowers, 1943

Oil on canvas, 82 × 55 cm
The Henry Lamb Estate

The artist's eldest child Henrietta arguably did more than any other member of his family to promote the work of Henry Lamb following his death in 1960. Described in her *Daily Telegraph* obituary as 'the most bookish of a bookish family',[9] she was educated at Godolphin School in Salisbury and at Somerville College, Oxford. Later in life she became a notable landscape gardener, her work helping to shape the look of Kensington and Chelsea. This included a long period on the committee of Ladbroke Square Gardens, in Notting Hill, one of the largest garden squares in London. Taking on the role of managing the Henry Lamb Estate she was unfailingly generous in allowing scholars access to the family's extensive archive and helping to facilitate the loan of works of art to exhibitions across the world. Perhaps by virtue of being two and eight years older than her respective siblings, she is possibly the most frequent sitter in her father's family portraits (with the exception of her mother). This full-length portrait of the twelve-year-old Henrietta is a striking depiction by a father of a daughter on the verge of adolescence.

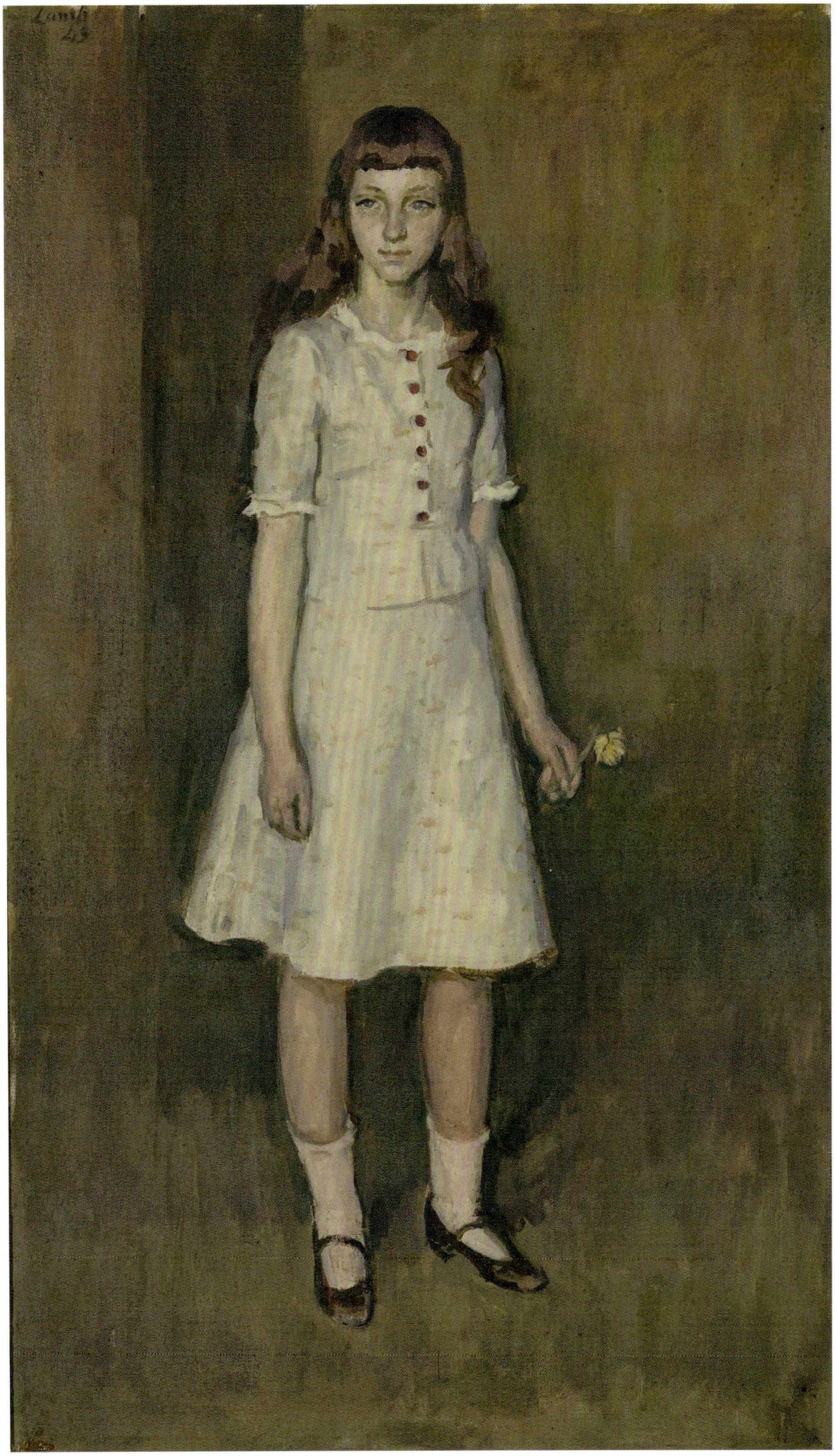

48

Clock Patience, 1949

Oil on canvas, 68 × 53 cm
Private collection

Clock Patience is the most intimate of Lamb's many paintings of card games, something of a favourite subject, with examples ranging from a wartime watercolour of troops playing cards in Salonika (dating from c.1918) to *Pub in Canning Town* (1928, location unknown) or its later version *Men at Cards* (cat. 49). It also forms part of a group of sensitive studies of his son Valentine, frequently depicted as if his young sitter is unknowingly in the presence of the artist. The artist's daughter Felicia recalls being paid sixpence per hour to keep Valentine occupied during his many long sittings, although by the date of this work, 1949, he was ten years old and probably capable of occupying himself (in this case intensely concentrating on his game). Valentine was a particularly frequent subject in paintings by Lamb, partly, the artist's daughter claims, due to their commercial success – pictures of Valentine were the family works that sold first.[10] A number of portraits of Valentine were also exhibited at the Royal Academy, including the present work in 1951 (no. 473).

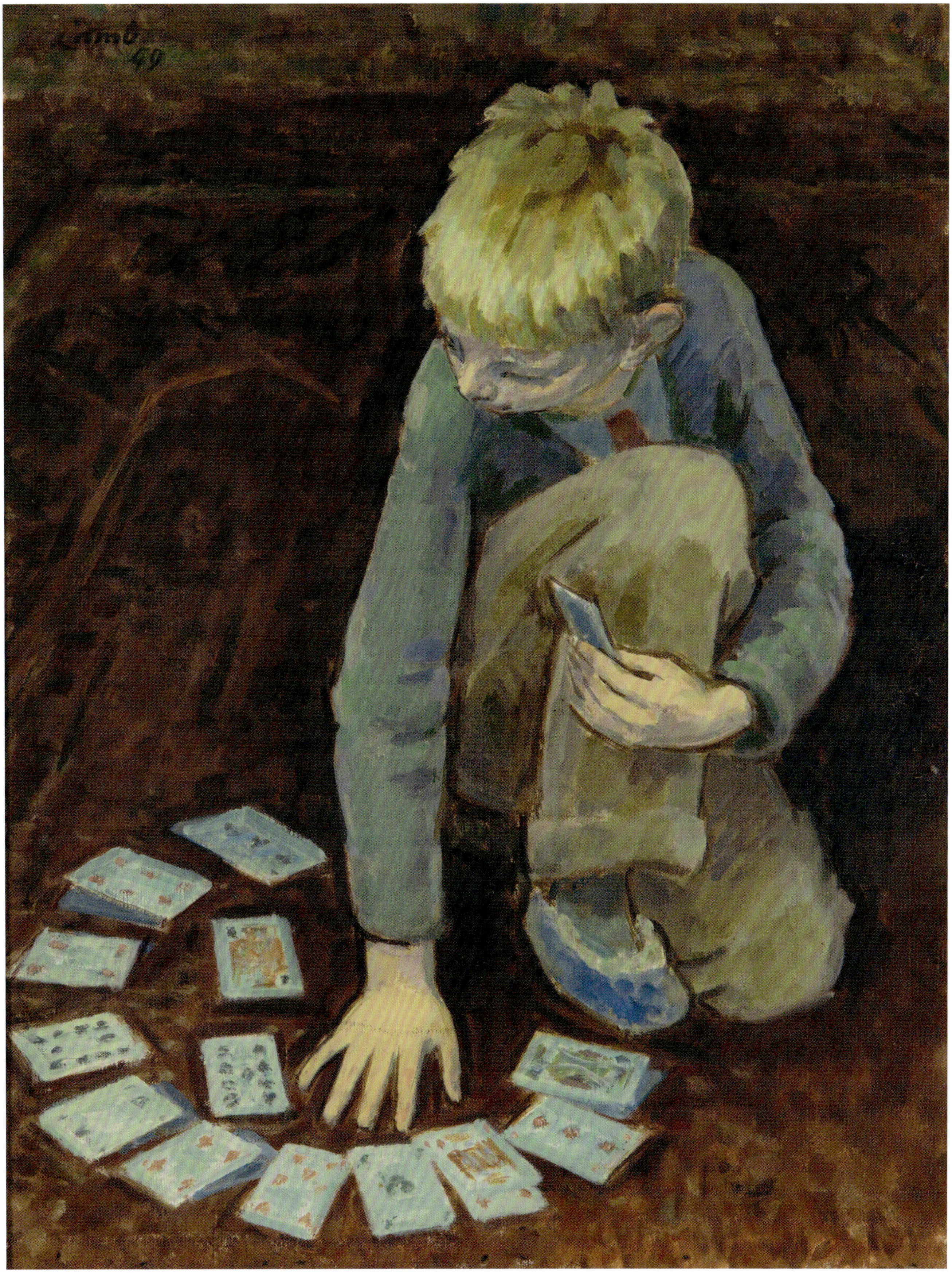

49

Men at Cards, c.1947

Oil on canvas, 72.5 × 63 cm
The Henry Lamb Estate

Illustrated in *Studio* in December 1947 and exhibited at the Royal Academy that year (no. 364), *Men at Cards* has at least one other near-identical version – an earlier painting titled *Pub in Canning Town* (location unknown), dating from 1928. It combines elements that occupied the artist's imagination at various periods in the 1920s in particular – most notably working-class subject paintings, the most successful example being the large work *Football Edition* (location unknown), which can at some level be viewed as a social commentary on the economic state of Poole. *Men at Cards* is a rare example of a London depiction of such a subject, the dark interior bearing some resemblance to the intense, brooding interior scenes of one of Lamb's first champions, Walter Sickert. Figures playing games, cards in particular, are a regular motif in Lamb's later work, including *The Card Players (Vingt et Un)* from 1952 (exhibited at the Leicester Galleries in 1956; private collection), which is a variant on the theme of the present painting, and *Clock Patience* (cat. 48).

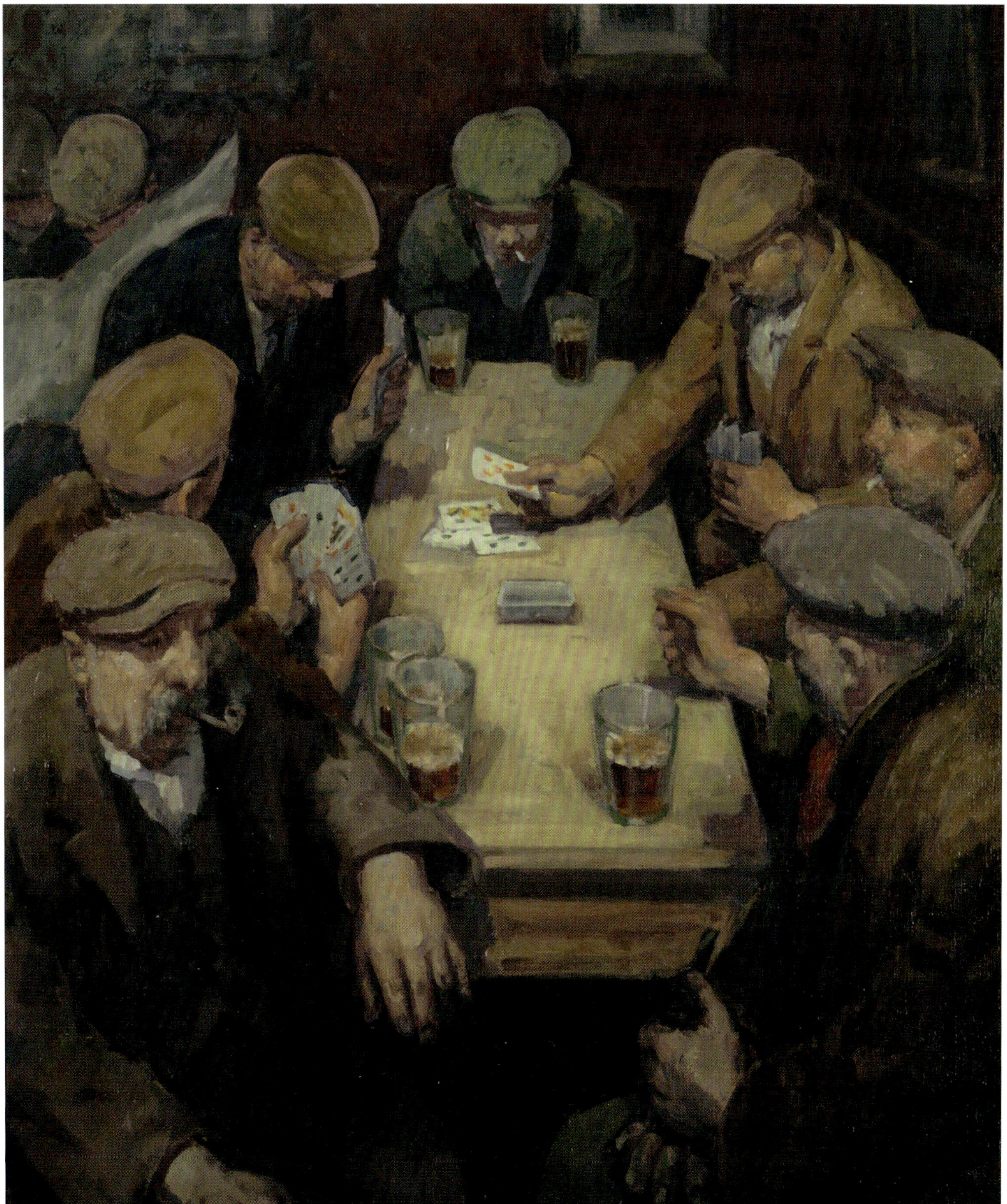

50

At the Cottage Door, 1940

Oil on board, 44.5 × 35 cm
The Henry Lamb Estate

This small figure painting is typical of the genre subjects Lamb would paint from the Second World War until his death. Although its location is unidentified, it is significant that Lamb travelled to Scotland in June 1940 as an external assessor to art colleges in Dundee, Aberdeen, Edinburgh and Glasgow, and it is plausibly a rural Scottish subject. Such rustic, almost primitive figure scenes attracted Lamb throughout his life, particularly in Brittany and Ireland, his experiences of which he would tellingly try to re-create from memory in his 'Souvenir' series of re-worked copies from the early 1950s (see cat. 51). The picture was in the collection of the artist's daughter Henrietta Phipps, and was exhibited at the *Artists of Fame and Promise* exhibition held at the Leicester Galleries in August 1960, a couple of months before the artist's death.

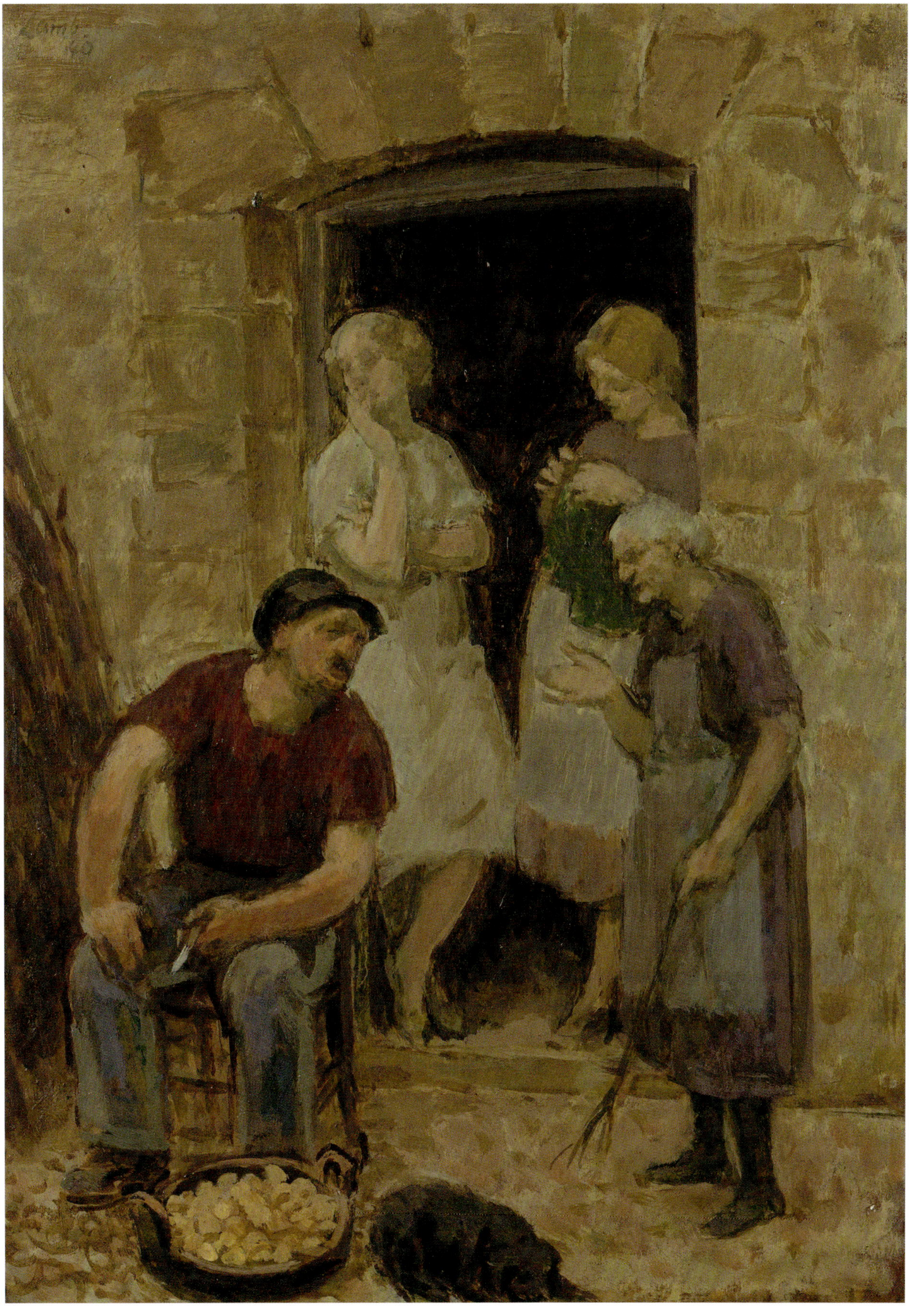

51

Mourners (Souvenir of Brittany, 1910), 1953

Oil on board, 74 × 58.5 cm
The Henry Lamb Estate

At the beginning of the 1950s Lamb began to return to some of the subjects and themes of his earlier career that had proved the most successful and enduring. Sometimes this included fresh material based on the example of earlier compositions, for example *Night Life* for the Festival of Britain in 1951 – a large nocturnal canvas showing young people on bicycles, a sort of conscious re-working of his idea for *Football Edition* in Poole back in 1926. In 1954 and 1955, though, he exhibited works at the Royal Academy Summer Exhibitions that can only really be classed as pure replicas – *Souvenir of Donegal* in 1955 (an almost exact re-working of *Fisherfolk*) and the present work in 1954 (no. 614). *Mourners* is a replica of the painting *Lamentation* (Tate), the second major work that dwelled on the death of Madame Favennec on his first visit to Doëlan in 1910. Although identical in composition, the present work, perhaps mitigated by the intervening 40 years, is noticeably softer in its rendering of the subjects' faces (particularly of the boy and the man to the front), and in general lacks the powerful intensity so apparent in the prime version.

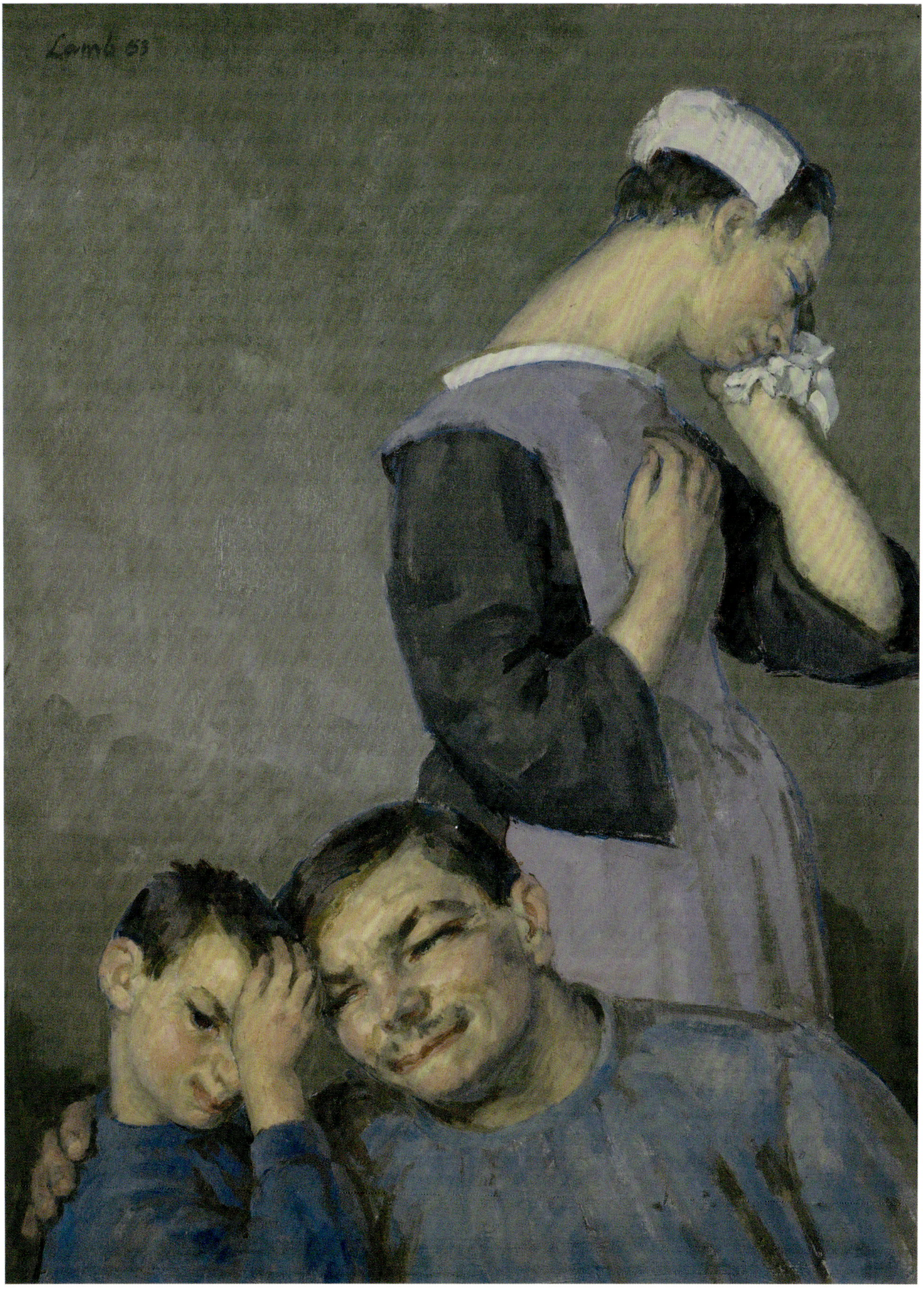
Lamb 53

CATALOGUE NOTES

EARLY WORKS

1 Quoted in Frances Spalding, 'The Self Portrait: A Cultural History – review', *The Guardian*, 27 March 2014.
2 The Manchester City Art Gallery catalogue from 1984, *Henry Lamb (1883–1960)*, dates the present drawing to c.1905, but bearing in mind the relative hesitancy of other drawings from that year and the fact that Lamb did not enroll in the Chelsea School of Art until early 1906, it seems unlikely that it would date from before this time. More plausible is that the strong pencil self-portraits from this date (despite slight variance in facial hair and style) were executed closer together than may first appear.
3 Keith Clements, *Henry Lamb, The Artist and his Friends*, Bristol 1985, p. 88.
4 'Of the contemporary foreign artists with whom he came into contact none seem to have had much influence ... unless perhaps Picasso ... the Breton youth here reproduced reflects it to a certain extent': G. L. Kennedy, *Contemporary British Artists: Henry Lamb*, London 1924, p. 14, pl. 3.
5 Clements 1985, p. 88, presumably based on conversations between Clements and surviving members of the Favennec family in the 1970s.
6 Henry Lamb to Lytton Strachey, 11 May 1911, Strachey Papers, British Library, vol. XX (fols. i–29).
7 Frank Rutter, *Evolution in Modern Art*, London 1926, p. 122.
8 This argument is convincingly made by Jonathan Meuli, 'Henry Lamb: A Survey of his Life and Work', unpublished BA diss., University of Cambridge (and Tate Gallery Archives) 1980.
9 *Henry Lamb (1883–1960)*, exh. cat., Manchester City Art Gallery, 1984, no. 21, p. 26.
10 Also known by the title *A Breton Shepherdess*, sold Sotheby's, London, *A Great British Collection: The Pictures collected by Sir David and Lady Scott, sold to benefit the Finnis Scott Foundation*, 19 November 2008, lot 185.
11 Henry Lamb to Lytton Strachey, 26 May 1911. See note 6 above for all Strachey correspondence.
12 Henry Lamb to Lytton Strachey, 11 May 1911.
13 Henry Lamb to Lytton Strachey, 24 July 1911.
14 Sold Christie's, *Modern British & Irish Art*, 26 June 2017, lot 2.
15 Henry Lamb to Lytton Strachey, 24 July 1911.
16 Henry Lamb to Lytton Strachey, 18 August 1911.
17 'The New English Art Club', *The Times*, 22 May 1911.
18 For further discussion of this portrait, see the Introduction to this catalogue, pp. 15–16.
19 'Review of the New English Art Club Exhibition', *The Times*, 25 May 1912.
20 Lady Pansy Lamb, in conversation with Keith Clements, suggested the work was painted when he was riding regularly, especially with Leonard Woolf, and that he had a fantasy about a white horse, especially one with wings.
21 Henry Lamb to Lytton Strachey, 22 September 1912.
22 Henry Lamb to Lytton Strachey, 22 August 1913.
23 Henry Lamb to Lytton Strachey, 30 August 1913.
24 Henry Lamb to Lytton Strachey, 11 October 1913.
25 Such as *Potato Pickers, Gola Island*, Sotheby's, London, *The Irish Sale*, 7 May 2008, lot 140.

WAR TO WAR

1 For a fuller discussion, see Paul Gough, *Stanley Spencer: Journey to Burghclere*, Bristol 2006
2 Quoted in Clements 1985, p. 227.
3 See Kennedy 1924, pl.23. This anecdote is also recalled in *Henry Lamb (1883–1960)* 1984, no. 58, p. 45.
4 There are also individual portrait studies for this work in the artist's sketchbooks, including one in blue ink inscribed by the artist Edgar McWilliam and clearly depicting the same sitter as the central figure in the present work.
5 There is some disagreement over the identity of the sitter in this work, the preliminary drawing for the painting in the Imperial War Museum identifying him as Corporal J. L. Nunn (see IWM.ART LD 1133).
6 Quoted in Clements 1985, p. 270.

FRIENDS AND RELATIONSHIPS, POOLE PERIOD

1 'The Cerne Giant is very surprising. How can he have survived?': Augustus John to Henry Lamb, 1912 (undated later), Tate Archive, TAM 15.
2 E-mail to the author from Michael Spender, Poole Museum, 19 January 2018.
3 'Lamb's splendid Paradise Street (Poole Museum) has an appealing picturesque quality based on the gothic effect of tall buildings ... it is a theme that recalls Sickert's Dieppe townscapes of 20 years earlier': Davies 1987, Ch. 3: 'Henry Lamb in Poole – 1922–1928', pp. 37ff.
4 Henry Lamb to Richard Carline, 4 April 1922, Tate Archive, 8212.1.1-29.
5 See Peter Davies, *Art in Poole & Dorset*, Poole 1987, p. 43, for a full discussion of this painting.
6 See Kennedy 1924, pl. 13.
7 '*A street, Poole Dorset* in Poole Museum – sweet Whistlerian panel ... women and children chatting on a street probably Lagland Street': Davies 1987, Ch. 3: 'Henry Lamb in Poole – 1922–1928', pp. 37ff.
8 This anecdote is referred to in Davies 1987, p. 50. It was related to the author by Lady Pansy Lamb during interviews with her in 1985.
9 An e-mail from David Watkins, Local History Manager at Poole Museum (20 January 2018), confirmed a visit in c.2009 from Mr Edenden's granddaughter Trisha Melvin, who further confirmed the identity of the sitters.
10 The table to the centre of this painting remained in the artist's possession following the family's move to Coombe Bissett, and the artist's daughter Felicia Palmer has confirmed that it is still in her possession today (telephone conversation with the author, 21 December 2017).
11 For example Henry Lamb to Richard Carline, 17 May 1924: 'Cookham and Hilda are the limit .... As far as I am concerned I have found the "upset of balance" to which you refer has greatly spoiled my interest in Cookham as a person', Tate Archive, 8212.1.1-29.
12 Michael Holroyd, *Augustus John*, Harmondsworth 1996, p. 359.
13 Quoted in Clements 1985, p. 62 (quotation not footnoted).
14 See *Henry Lamb (1883–1960)* 1984, no. 50, p. 42.

15 Kennedy 1924, p. 12.
16 See the entry on this work in *Henry Lamb (1883–1960)* 1984, no. 62, p. 48.
17 From 'The Composition', quoted in Bryan Guinness, *Potpourri from the Thirties*, Albuquerque 1982, p. 18.
18 John Fothergill, *An Innkeeper's Diary*, London 1931, p. 229, quoted Clements 1985, p. 267.
19 'I am at present staying with Henry Lamb who is painting my portrait and delivering illuminating discourses on Cezanne': Evelyn Waugh to Harold Acton (Letters, p. 27), quoted in *Henry Lamb (1883–1960)* 1984, no. 68, p. 50.
20 Ibid.
21 Henry Lamb to Evelyn Waugh, 14 August 1929, Evelyn Waugh Papers, vol. xv, British Library, Add MS 81060: 1929-1965.
22 Henry Lamb to Evelyn Waugh, 25 May 1948, ibid.
23 Sold Christie's, South Kensington, *Modern British & Irish Art*, 9 December 2015, lot 31.
24 'Royal Academy Stage Pictures', *The Stage*, 6 May 1937.
25 For further discussion see Geoffrey Miller, *The Bournemouth Symphony Orchestra*, 1970.
26 'Bournemouth Curator and Sir Dan Godfrey's portrait', *Bournemouth Echo*, 2 April 1937.
27 *Punch*, 12 May 1937, p. 517.

PEACE, HOME AND FAMILY

1 *Exhibition of works by Henry Lamb*, Leicester Galleries, April–May 1927, no. 87.
2 In the collection of the artist's family.
3 Old Rowley Fine Art Auctioneers, May 27 2008, lot 384.
4 I am very grateful to Laura Grace Simpkins of Messums Wiltshire for this observation as well as other information from her extensive note on the painting for Messums Wiltshire in 2017.
5 Quoted Clements 1985, p. 263.
6 Anthony Powell, *Messenger of Day, The Memoirs of Anthony Powell*, vol. 2, New York, 1978, p. 70, quoted Clements 1985, p. 263.
7 Clements 1985, p. 279.
8 Letter from Ian McKenzie Smith (director of Aberdeen Gallery and Museums Department) to Spink & Sons Ltd., 12 September 1980.
9 *The Daily Telegraph*, 'Henrietta Phipps', Obituary, 24 June 2016.
10 As told told to the author in a telephone call to the artist's daughter, Felicia Palmer, 21 December 2017.

SELECTED LITERATURE

A Memorial Exhibition of Paintings, Drawings and Watercolours by Henry Lamb, exh. cat., Leicester Galleries, 1961 (introduction by William Gaunt)

Mark Amory (ed.), *The Letters of Evelyn Waugh*, London 2010

Wendy Baron, *The Camden Town Group*, London 1979

Keith Clements, *Henry Lamb, The Artist and his Friends*, Bristol 1985

Peter Davies, *Art in Poole and Dorset*, Poole 1987

Nicolette Devas, *Two Flamboyant Fathers*, London 1966

Brian Foss, '"No Dead Wood": Henry Lamb and the Canadians', *Canadian Military History*, vol. 6, issue 2, 2012

Paul Gough, *Stanley Spencer, Journey to Burghclere*, Bristol 2006

Bryan Guinness, *Potpourri from the Thirties*, Albuquerque 1982

David Boyd Haycock, *A Crisis of Brilliance, Five Young British Artists and the Great War*, London 2009

Henry Lamb (1883–1960), exh. cat., Manchester City Art Gallery, 1984 (with contributions by Anthony Powell, Keith Clements and Sandra Martin)

Michael Holroyd, *Lytton Strachey and the Bloomsbury Group*, Harmondsworth 1971

Michael Holroyd, *Augustus John*, Harmondsworth 1976 (1st edn 1974)

G.L. Kennedy, *Henry Lamb*, London 1924

Geoffrey Miller, *The Bournemouth Symphony Orchestra*, Wincanton 1970

Jonathan Meuli, 'Henry Lamb: A Survey of his Life and Work', unpublished BA diss., University of Cambridge (and Tate Gallery Archives) 1980

Anthony Powell, *Messenger of Day, The Memoirs of Anthony Powell*, New York 1978

John Rothenstein, *British Artists and the War*, London 1931

Frank Rutter, *Some Contemporary Artists*, London 1922

Frank Rutter, *Evolution in Modern Art*, London 1926

Richard Shone, *The Art of Bloomsbury*, London 2002

John Spencer (ed.), *Stanley Spencer, Looking to Heaven*, London 2016

PHOTOGRAPHIC CREDITS

CATALOGUE IMAGES

Cat. 1 Image © Ashmolean Museum, University of Oxford (WA1956.43)

Cat. 2, 11, 15, 24, 27, 29–30, 33–34, 39, 44, 46, 48 Private collection. Photography by Owen Smith and Bill Gore

Cat. 3, 9 © Courtesy of the Henry Lamb Estate / Bridgeman Images

Cat. 4, 10 © Tate, London 2017

Cat. 5, 7, 13, 21, 36–38, 41–43, 45, 47, 49–51 © The Henry Lamb Estate. Photography by Owen Smith and Bill Gore

Cat. 6 © Manchester Art Gallery

Cat. 8 © Henry Lamb Estate. Photo credit: Homerton College, Cambridge

Cat. 12 © National Portrait Gallery, London

Cat. 14 ©IWM (Art.IWM ART LD 2746)

Cat. 16 ©IWM (Art.IWM ART LD 1143)

Cat. 17 ©IWM (Art.IWM ART LD 1137)

Cat. 18 Photograph kindly reproduced with the permission of the Russell-Cotes Art Gallery & Museum, Bournemouth

Cat. 19 ©IWM (Art.IWM ART LD 429)

Cat. 20 ©IWM (Art.IWM ART LD 3206)

Cat. 22 ©IWM (Art.IWM ART LD 1139)

Cat. 23–26, 28 © Poole Museum

Cat. 31 ©Manchester Art Gallery / Bridgeman Images

Cat. 32 The Hon. Daphne Guinness. Photography by Owen Smith and Bill Gore

Cat. 35 © Henry Lamb Estate / Photograph kindly reproduced with the permission of the Russell-Cotes Art Gallery & Museum, Bournemouth

Cat. 40 Courtesy of Messum's Wiltshire, representatives of the Henry Lamb Estate. Photography Iain Kemp

COMPARATIVE IMAGES

Fig. 1, 11 © Tate, London 2018

Figs. 2, 3, 4, 10, 12–13 © Henry Lamb Estate. Photography by Owen Smith and Bill Gore

Fig. 5 © Courtesy of the Henry Lamb Estate/ Bridgeman Images. Photo © Christie's Images/Bridgeman Images

Fig. 6 Photo credit: Jonathan Clark Fine Art

Fig. 7 © De Agostini Picture Library / G. Dagli Orti / Bridgeman Images

Fig. 8 © Stanley Spencer Estate

Fig. 9 Private Collection. Photography by Owen Smith and Bill Gore